Sidelined By your Adult Children?

Sidelined By your Adult Children?

HOW TO TAKE CHARGE AND BE HAPPY

Rosanne Rosen and Dr. Patricia James Ph.D.

ISBN: 1517398061
ISBN 13: 9781517398064
Library of Congress Control Number: 2015915471
CreateSpace Independent Publishing Platform
North Charleston, South Carolina

Table of Contents

A Must-Read Introduction

A huge part of our lives has been focused on raising our children, worrying about them, saving for college, pleasing them, and making sure they liked us. When solving problems with our children, we have been concerned about pleasing them.

Well, it's time someone considered moms and dads!

Sidelined by Your Adult Children? How to Take Charge and Be Happy is a parent-centered book.

It concentrates on those of us who became parents from the mid-sixties to the early nineties and on our relationship with these now-adult children. **We, their parents, are the sidelined generation.**

A review of self-help articles and books reveals lists of accommodating suggestions for parents to improve relationships with their adult children: keep quiet, don't offer advice, never criticize, endure whatever behavior they dish out, and avoid conflict at all costs. These recommendations are fine if you're satisfied being a voiceless marionette whose strings are pulled by your children. In our professional opinion, there is a much healthier path for parents to follow that can ensure happiness among sidelined parents relegated to a less-than-fulfilling position in their children's lives.

It is time to start worrying about you!

Our goal is to free you from the lopsided effect your adult children have upon your state of mind and level of personal happiness. After carefully reading parts I and II, you will understand the dynamics of the syndrome we have termed "sidelining" and be ready to master the techniques prescribed to get past its effects. Your reward will be replacing anger, pain, aggravation, sadness, and disappointment with contentment, self-satisfaction, inner peace, and a better relationship with your adult children.

Committing to being happy will enable you to approach the ideas in this book with an open mind, a willing heart, and an eager attitude. You may not initially agree with everything you read. You will need to:

- Be able to laugh and see humor in some of the antics of your adult children
- Accept that neither you nor your adult child is always right or always wrong
- Take responsibility for your own feelings and actions
- Work hard, experiment, and accept new points of view
- Accept that life doesn't always work out just the way you want it to

How do I know this approach works? It has made me an entirely new person! Whether or not my children would agree with that is irrelevant. My happiness quotient verifies the truthfulness of my statement, and my confidence in the wisdom in this book makes me brave enough to suggest to my daughters that they read what we have written. ***Rosanne Rosen***

<u>Important Note Regarding Format:</u>

<u>References to **I**,</u> *other than those noted in quoted anecdotes, signify Rosanne Rosen's personal views and experiences.*

<u>References to **Pat**,</u> *highlight the professional views of Dr. Patricia James, PH.D.*

<u>References to **We**,</u> *other than those noted in quoted anecdotes, indicate the joint research, findings and opinions of both Rosanne Rosen and Dr. Patricia James.*

How to Use This Guide

*S*idelined by Your Adult Children? How to Take Charge and Be Happy was thoughtfully written to make you a happier, healthier parent and individual. The progression of the chapters prepares you for the personal discoveries necessary to get out from under the emotional ups and downs caused by hurtful interactions with your adult children. You need to start at the beginning, read every chapter in the order given, absorb each new concept, and advance from one step to the next as presented to you.

Taking charge of your life is most successful when you approach this task in an orderly manner. Understanding the sidelining syndrome we have uncovered, achieving valuable realizations, and finding the happy place you wish to dwell in is a process that cannot be rushed. There is no one-size-fits-all answer. To arrive at your personal solution requires your active participation.

Part 1–The Reality of Sidelining

Sidelining is a complex issue that goes way beyond a generational divide. Consequently, before we plunge into what you can do for yourself, we need to thoroughly introduce you to the sidelining syndrome.

Sidelining, a new phenomenon affecting countless parents who are totally frustrated with their adult children, is widespread and troublesome; it is a wonderment these parents haven't taken to the streets picketing for better treatment. Pat (Dr. James) has called some of the scenarios tearfully recounted by these parents' examples of reverse child abuse!

To make things perfectly clear, we are talking about adult children whose parents did everything to help them grow up. These were dedicated and self-sacrificing parents who adored their kids.

For the parents who bravely bared their stories and feelings, the process was a way to vent their frustration and search for new insights. Their painful secrets enabled us to formulate a clear pattern of the behaviors and feelings that give light to the syndrome we named sidelining.

Identifying a pattern of behavior prevalent enough to qualify as a syndrome is only part of the issue. Gleaning more understanding of the social forces affecting the relationship between parents and their adult children is equally critical. Sidelining is also born out of different kinds of personalities, circumstances, grievances misunderstandings, upbringing, and expectations.

A warning must accompany Part I of the book.

Some of these anecdotes can be quite upsetting. Do not allow these horror tales, trials, or tribulations described by fellow parents to upset and anger you to the extent that you miss the point of these testimonies. Rather, accept the fact that you aren't alone, and see if you recognize yourself in their relationships. You might have insightful revelations that impact your thoughts about your own sidelining experiences.

CHAPTER 1

The Sidelining Syndrome

The object of Chapter 1 is not to engage in child bashing!

Enough of that has already been done, serving no end other than creating grief, disappointment, and disillusionment. However, it is absolutely imperative that we present a clear picture of the behavior that describes sidelining.

A large majority of the moms and dads who filled out our surveys or consented to interviews in Pat's office, on the phone, at restaurants, or in their homes experienced some form of sidelining. They just didn't know what to call it or that so many of their peers shared their woes.

Defining Sidelining

There have always been troubled scenarios within families. Classical scholars found complaints by both parents and older children in Sumerian texts dating as far back as 2100 to 1550 BC. And American heroine Eleanor Roosevelt admitted that her adult children's behavior drove her to consider suicide.

It is normal and natural to become irritated and feel tension with those close to you. This is intensified between parents and adult children because of the unique length and nature of their emotional attachment. Nonetheless, past generations of adult children more typically displayed outward signs of behavior congruent with love, respect, consideration, and admiration for parents whom they believed possessed wisdom from which they could learn. The extended family was of primary importance and value. Family gatherings were a time for fun. Visits were once warm, welcoming, and loving.

Things have changed!

To be sidelined is to experience behavior directed toward you by your adult child that makes you feel marginalized, diminished, disregarded, or disrespected.

When sidelining occurs often and repeatedly, it not only impedes the possibility to build a happy relationship but also intensifies misunderstandings, escalates grievances, fuels flames of dissatisfaction, and perpetuates a damaging cycle of interaction that can do irreparable, long-term harm to the adult child–parent relationship. There is, however, a constructive way to deal with sidelining that can liberate you from your pain, increase your happiness, and constructively impact your relationship with your adult children, which is precisely the goal of this book!

Images of Sidelining

Forget for a moment what is causing the difficulty. This examination is to uncover what sidelining looks like. The behavior may run the gamut from a curt remark to total estrangement. **Not all sidelining is done intentionally or even consciously, nor is it received the same way among parents.**

Sidelining is a combination of behavior, perception, reaction, and response.

Everyday Examples of Sidelining

Commonplace, everyday examples of sidelining are simple, insensitive behaviors that can be hurtful. Nearly 99 percent of parents admitted to being on the receiving end of these or similar thoughtless acts.

Here are a few examples reported in the words of parents in our study:

1) "Oh, it's you again. What do you want this time?" Becky said, answering her mother's phone call.

2) "What are *you* doing here?" asked an obviously annoyed daughter-in-law upon opening her front door to greet her husband's parents.

3) When asked by his mother to bring his children to visit over a long weekend break from school, this son replied, "Why? What would the kids do there?"

4) "My daughter called and asked if I would pay for the children's after-school classes. I had just sent money for her car payment. When I hesitated, she became angry. The next weekend was Mother's Day; I never received a call or a card."

Moderately Intense Sidelining

Well over 50 percent of our participants described incidents of more intense sidelining that constituted inexcusable, inconsiderate behavior that demonstrated little or no regard for them as valued individuals and parents.

Read their examples:

1) "I went to take care of my grandchildren for a week while their parents took a vacation. When my daughter returned and inspected the house, I was told there was spoiled food in the refrigerator. I was dismissed like a hired sitter without so much as a thank-you," complained one grandmother.

2) "It's like I don't exist anymore," this single dad explained. "I did everything I could for my daughter—college, a wedding, and trips. Now I don't get even a birthday card or a phone call. When I ask her what's wrong, she turns my words around and says, 'You're whining.'"

3) "I couldn't believe it," Fred admitted, referring to his son's behavior. "Our family was so close. I had no complaints about my son before now. Danny, his wife, and two kids came to town and stayed with his in-laws, who live about twenty minutes away from us. He never bothered to tell us he was in town and didn't bother to call us or come see us even once! Then he went to one of our favorite family restaurants with his kids and father-in-law to carry on the tradition without me."

4) "My son can get very angry. He can cut me to the quick like a stranger or send me a hideous note if I say anything he doesn't like. But his in-laws can say and do anything. I feel abused."

5) "My husband and I attended a family wedding. My son and his wife were there as well. The weekend-long event took place in Chicago, providing an opportunity for the four of us, who live fifteen hundred miles from each other, to spend time together. Instead my son booked a hotel away from where our family and the wedding guests were staying. The cost of the rooms was not an issue. I guess we were. During the entire weekend, the only moments I had with my son were at the wedding."

Repetitious Sidelining

No one who described being sidelined had only one example to offer. What did vary among these individuals were the degree, frequency, and duration of the sidelining incidents. Once a pattern of sidelining is established, it easily slides into a modus operandi that puts both parents and adult children on guard.

1) A case of multiple offenses

"I have to jump through hoops to get time with my grandchildren. I could have plans and will get a text from my daughter shortly before we are to meet saying she has to cancel.

"If it's not broken plans, then it's something else.

"A few years ago, we had terrible snowstorms. I happened to be at her house, which is a good forty minutes from where I live by myself. I hinted that it would be great for me to spend the night. She ignored me completely.

"That was easier to take than when I asked if I could join their family vacation for a few days. Without hesitation, she emphatically said, 'No!'

"More recently, I had knee replacement surgery. My daughter came to the hospital while I was being operated on. Then I didn't see her for ten days. I live alone and could have used her help."

2) A case of being endlessly sidelined

"For two years, we have been trying to plan a family trip. No matter what dates we come up with, my son always calls and says it won't work. Nothing ever works!

"My own son told me to stay home for Thanksgiving dinner and then come to visit his family for the weekend. His in-laws only wanted their family for the holiday, so we weren't invited.

"When I do visit and stay at their home, I am criticized for everything I do, even the way I put the dishes in the dishwasher.

"My daughter-in-law and I got into an argument. My son was furious. So was his wife. He called me and told me never to f——ing talk to his wife like that again. A few weeks later, she called my husband and invited him to our granddaughter's violin recital. It was made clear that I was not welcome to attend."

Situational Sidelining

There are cases when parents who have nice relationships with their adult offspring find themselves sidelined because of specific situations that have arisen.

Case #1

"I have been very close to my boys and relied on their opinions for everything until I met a man who was really wonderful to me. When I decided to live with him, it changed my relationship with them completely. They never invited him to a family party or holiday or allowed me to bring my grandchildren to our home. I was so disappointed in my kids; they were cold and constantly disapproving. I didn't enjoy being around any of them. It was one of the worst times in my life.

"When my companion died suddenly and tragically, my boys were there for me and have been ever since."

Case #2

Sally, her daughter, and her teenage granddaughter were going to attend a family gathering out of town. It was understood that Sally, who has a moderate income, would pay for the hotel. A day before their departure, her daughter upgraded their accommodations to a hotel with an indoor pool and reserved a second room for herself and her husband who suddenly decided to come along.

Too uncomfortable to cancel and unwilling to forego the time with her granddaughter, Sally went along with the changes. When asked how the weekend went, Sally said, "Awful. I'm the one who felt used and abused, more like an intruder with deep pockets."

Case #3

Cynthia and Tom decided to give their daughter a sum of money to purchase a condominium. Instead of a thank-you, they were told the money wasn't enough to cover the type of place she had in mind. For a year, their daughter was distant and chilly until they upped the ante.

The Absolute Ten of Sidelining

In each of the following cases, an adult child has chosen not to have a relationship with his or her parents.

It is very sad for the parents, Pat says, and hard to accept. Generally it seems there isn't much that can be done to change the relationship.

According to Dr. Joshua Coleman, psychologist and author of *When Parents Hurt*, estrangement by adult children is on the rise with parents who have been diligent and caring and had previously satisfying relationships. The causes of the downfall generally include conflicts related to money, boyfriends, partners, parental divorce, or remarriage.

Substance abuse is also a major cause of deteriorated relationships and is often an invisible factor.

A Grieving Mother

"My daughter was doted on and loved, although by her teens, it was apparent she had serious problems. We got her good therapy and have always been at her side. Still, no matter what I did when she was younger or now that she is in her forties, it backfires. If you piss her off, you are done.

"She asked my advice on a home she was thinking of buying and decided my body language was negative. As a result, she became all icy and stopped talking to me for a while. Then she wanted my opinion on whether she should ask her ex-husband for increased child support. I told her I thought they had an amicable divorce, which was important, and it seemed like he was doing all he should.

"Since then, she has spoken to me three times in the last five years. She didn't come to my mother's funeral or her grandfather's memorial service. I wish we were on a different path, but we aren't."

A Cast-Off Dad

"I never thought my firstborn, Sam, wouldn't speak to me. But that's what happened fourteen years ago after he met a woman he wanted to marry. My wife and I flew out west to meet her and make plans for the rehearsal dinner. It wasn't very long until tensions arose, and our relationship began to deteriorate.

"First of all, I was accused of being prejudiced because we took our son, his fiancée, and her parents, who are part Mexican American, to a Southwestern restaurant for dinner. And then the e-mail arrived that began the war," Robert said. "Sam thinks we have very deep pockets. He asked if I would I pay for the wine and alcohol at the wedding. I responded that I would not and included a list of all we were willing to do: pay for a lovely rehearsal dinner, give them a nice check for a wedding gift, and cover the cost of a honeymoon.

"In Sam's e-mail before the wedding, we were told not to attend unless we were on our best behavior. Of course we went. Our extended family showed up gracious and smiling. Sam was rude and mean spirited to everyone, even his grandparents whom he ignored entirely.

"After the honeymoon, I received another nasty e-mail in which Sam outlined my character defects."

In our opinion, Robert did not appear to be afflicted by any serious character defects. Sam, however, probably suffer from ongoing sibling rivalry related to unequal amounts of money gifted by his parents. Sam thinks he is entitled to more of his father's resources and feels cheated when he doesn't get what he thinks he should have.

"I waited a year for an apology. We spoke one time after that and haven't been in touch for thirteen years."

Abandoned Mom and Grandmother

"I can hardly talk about it," said Joy who still finds the lengthy estrangement from her daughters and grandchildren physically painful.

"I divorced my husband because he was abusive. I never told my girls why we separated. I wanted to spare them the real details about their father. I raised them myself with little interaction with their father. When they got into their mid-twenties, they each started a relationship with him and then decided to have nothing to do with me.

"They still don't. I have seen them just a few times in ten years. Reconciliation was attempted once but failed. I was informed by e-mail that they no longer wanted to see me."

Common Behaviors and Attitudes of Sidelining

Interviews and questionnaires revealed the most common behaviors and attitudes associated with adult children who sideline. The list compiled below further illuminates sidelining.

Adult children who sideline parents are:

- Uncommunicative
- Dismissive

- Judgmental
- Cold
- Controlling
- Punishing
- Unforgiving
- Rude
- Disrespectful
- Unwelcoming
- Distant
- Unsympathetic
- Unloving
- Uncaring
- Hostile
- Evasive
- Unkind

Positive Sidelining

While we strongly advocate finding ways to make a child-parent relationship work, there are circumstances when an adult child engages in positive or healthy sidelining. If a parent's behavior has the potential to be emotionally damaging, it may be better to steer clear of mom and dad. We think the young woman who told us this story had just cause to do that.

"My mom was a negligent parent and alcoholic. I got into drugs and all kinds of trouble. I finally left home and straightened myself out. Two years ago, when I was twenty-three, I took a day off of work to go see my mother. I drove four hours to get to her home. The date and time were set. I arrived, and she wasn't there. When I finally reached her, she said she was with her boyfriend, and it wasn't a good time to get together. I knew then that the toxicity of my mother's behavior was hazardous to my mental and physical health and that I shouldn't keep working on having a relationship with her."

You and Sidelining

Now that you have a better picture of what constitutes sidelining, make your own list of grievances. It will provide a handy reference for later. Can you list ten instances when your adult children sidelined you?

1. _____

2. _____

3. _____

4. _____

5. _____

6. _____

7. _____

8. _____

9. _____

10. _____

You may also want to circle any of the following sidelining tactics reported by other parents that apply to you.

My adult children do the following:

- Fail to answer the phone when I call
- Frequently refuse my invitations for meals, outings, or vacations together
- Often speak to me in ways I feel are disrespectful

- Fail to invite me to my grandchildren's school events
- Act as if I am an embarrassment or annoyance
- Take advantage of my time and money
- Forget to acknowledge the nice things I did for them
- Treat me like a second-class citizen, an enemy, an intruder, or a stranger
- Rarely find time to spend with me
- Celebrate my birthday, Mother's Day, or Father's Day as an afterthought
- Tell me how to behave in their house
- Show more consideration to their in-laws than me
- Show little interest in my being an integral part of their lives
- Extend little empathy or understanding toward me
- Behave as if I am someone who has no feelings and needs to be tolerated
- Infrequently ask my opinion or advice on important matters
- Rarely include me in their lives
- Tolerate nasty or disrespectful behavior toward me by their spouses

What's Next?

We have carefully drawn a vivid picture of the syndrome we call sidelining in order for you to begin identifying your reaction to it. However, this isn't all we have to say about the characteristics of sidelining. Don't stop here, even though you may be comforted for the moment knowing that you aren't alone. A more complex picture will emerge as we go about the serious business of helping you take charge of your responses to sidelining.

For the moment, however, let's look at how our study participants reacted to sidelining. You may find their behavior similar to your own. Eventually we will provide you with insights and strategies that are more effective and advantageous to regaining your happiness while building a better relationship with your adult children.

CHAPTER 2

The Sting of Being Sidelined

There is no denying that the impact of sidelining upon caring, well-intentioned parents can be painful and harmful in both a physical and an emotional sense. Identifying how sidelining affects other parents can be useful in illuminating your own responses.

Not all parents react the same way. Some have a particular sensitivity to being sidelined and are strongly affected. Others are less severely troubled. Determining how you respond should be the first item on your agenda.

Accepting Cold, Hard Facts

There are a number of important truths that need to be out in the open, on the table and accepted by parents of adult children today. There is no hidden blame in this section. These are important facts that need to be ingested in order to begin your quest for personal happiness when confronted with sidelining kids.

Fact #1: Parents tend to hold a relationship ideal that is not shared by many in their adult children's generation.

Fact #2: Parents frequently want more than their adult kids are willing to give. It often seems to be the case that parents feel more connected to their kids and place more value in their relationship with them than their offspring do.

Fact #3: You cannot impose the relationship you desire on anyone—child, spouse, friend, or family member. Nor can you dictate how someone reacts to you or demand they love or like you.

Fact #4: The adult child–parent relationship naturally embodies some degree of tension. Mothers and fathers both find more tension in their relationships with daughters than with sons. Both sons and daughters, on the other hand, experience more tension with their moms than their dads.

Fact #5: There is a correlation between the degree to which parents were vested in their children and the emotional pain of being sidelined. Pat's years of clinical experience confirm that the greater the level of being vested in raising children, the more intense the feelings and reactions to being sidelined are.

Summarizing Thoughts and Feelings Experienced from Sidelining

Pain, anger, unloved, disgusted, alienated, hurt, annoyed, mistreated, cheated, dumped, frustrated, sad, diminished, distrusted, empty, disappointed, incompetent, excluded, and *unneeded* are words used by both mothers and fathers to describe how they felt when sidelined.

Now, go through the following list, and put a big check mark by the words that describe what you feel when sidelined.

- Pain
- Anger
- Unloved
- Disgusted
- Alienated
- Hurt
- Annoyed
- Mistreated

- Cheated
- Dumped
- Frustrated
- Sad
- Diminished
- Distrusted
- Empty
- Disappointed
- Incompetent
- Excluded
- Unneeded
- Disregarded
- Marginalized
- Disrespected
- Invisible

Add your own thoughts in case we missed something you have felt.

1) _____

_____

2) _____

_____

3) _____

_____

4) _____

_____

5) _____

_____

The Complexity of Feeling Sidelined

The reactions one feels when sidelined are multifaceted.

Let's look at Jane and her Mother's Day gift, a lunch invitation from her son.

She finally asked him in September, "You know that lunch out? When is it going to happen?"

She admits to feeling angry at this point.

He responded, "You know mom I have been really busy."

"At 2:00 a.m. that night, I sent him an e-mail that read, 'I am very sad. In four months, you haven't had time for lunch.'

"When we finally got together, I couldn't relax and be myself. He showed no interest in what I was doing. He didn't ask me one question. It was hurtful.

"Things didn't end well. I said his father and I would like to hear from him more often."

He replied, "Whatever I give you, you want more."

"You are right," she told him, feeling excluded and unloved.

"Maybe our relationship isn't fixable," she wondered out loud to us. "But I hoped it could be better."

How Parents Respond to Sidelining

Patterns of behavior emerged with some regularity from our study. Unfortunately many responses did little to discourage further sidelining. You will have the benefit of learning from these errors.

Knee-Jerk Reactions

The immediate response to the sting of being sidelined is often pure emotion. This reaction can be quick, unfiltered, and irrational, with damaging effects that long outlast the moment.

Unfortunately, very few individuals can, in the heat of an extremely emotionally tense or hurtful moment, avoid an uncensored reaction 100 percent of the time.

Sidelined parents admit to doing the following:

1) Going stone-cold silent
2) Hanging up on their adult kids
3) Stomping out of the house
4) Getting into a shouting match
5) Saying things they wish they hadn't

The first three actions on the list are the least damaging but still not advisable. The last two on the list are the ones that can get you into real trouble, do nothing to rid you of angst or unhappiness, and are the responses you want to avoid.

These behaviors can reflect the following:

- The inability to manage reactions when totally disgusted, frustrated, or angry
- The tendency to protect oneself
- The desire to strike back and be vindictive or hurtful

If you make a habit of knee-jerk reactions, they are one of the first things you need to take charge of.

Personal-Injury Responses
More subtle reactions to feeling sidelined do not fuel wildfires, but they can be seriously damaging to your health, happiness, and well-being. If your reaction resembles any of those listed below and is of a lengthy duration, your risk of personal injury is high!

Ask yourself if you engage in these potentially injurious personal responses noted by other parents:

Responses	Yes	No
1) Brooding		
2) Forming quiet new grudges		
3) Self-pitying		
4) Acting like a victim		
5) Harboring resentments		
6) Viewing oneself as a failure		
7) Avoiding adult children		
8) Shutting down communication		
9) Arguing with your spouse		
10) Going on the defense		
11) Becoming depressed		
12) Denying authentic feelings		
13) Walking on eggshells		

What Personal-Injury Cases Look Like

A few examples ought to clarify what we mean.

Case #1

"I can just crumble when I am not getting along with my kids. I absolutely have to go to bed."

Case #2

"My priorities must be the exact opposite of my daughter's. I would love to have dinner with her family once a week or celebrate a special birthday with an extended family getaway. I can't even get my daughter to agree to have lunch with me every now and then. After being with friends who talk about doing all kinds of wonderful things with their children and grandkids, I feel sad. I want to go home and hide in bed. Most of the time I just carry on my day sulking and feeling sorry for myself."

Case #3

"Our daughter lives two blocks away and always has an excuse and nasty attitude about why it isn't a good time to come over and pick up our granddaughters. My wife used to regularly babysit for her when the girls were younger. Now they have no time for her. She is depressed and stays at home."

Case #4

"My husband never tells our children what he thinks or how they make him feel.

"Sometimes I am afraid he is going to explode with all the anger he keeps inside. There is no discussing this with him. The last time he became overly aggravated after a family dinner, he sped away from our daughter's house like he was running away from a terrorist. He is normally a careful, respectful driver. We bounced over a bump so high I thought the undercarriage of the car was going to be damaged.

"His main complaint is that it is just assumed we will do everything for our adult children—run car pools, help out in a pinch, and pay for dinners in restaurants. I guess he feels they take advantage of him and says it's time the tables turned a little. He never gets a thank-you for the little or big things he does. And I have to admit, he does a lot and groans a lot.

"This particular night, the kids had just come back from visiting the in-laws, whom they expect very little from. I cooked and took dinner over so that we could see our grandchildren and make things easy for our daughter. While we were consuming the meal I had made, we sat there hearing about all the lovely things she and her husband did for the in-laws and the places they took them to. Then we were told they were sorry, but they wouldn't be in town for Father's Day next month. They were going to go back to the in-laws. When we were leaving, our daughter told me she put her twin boys' birthday wish list in the sack with the empty bowls of food."

Mothers and Fathers Don't Always React the Same

On the whole, mothers tend to be more affected by their relationship with their adult children than do fathers. That doesn't mean, however, that sidelining doesn't grievously influence men. Primarily, they react in different ways.

Forgive and Forget

Mothers seem to forgive and forget long before fathers do. These examples note this typical difference.

Moms

"My daughter doesn't take criticism very well. I could tone down a little or be more gentle," Laura admits. "She gets angry with me. If she answers me in a way I don't care for, being nippy or argumentative, I just say good-bye and hang up. We might get mad for a few days, maybe even a couple of weeks, and not talk. Afterward, to be honest, I don't even remember the context of the call. It's just what we do."

Laura's ability to forgive and forget was fairly common among mothers who didn't have serious issues with their children. On the other hand, we found only one father who displayed this tendency.

Dads

Helen and Jay agreed that Paul was making their lives miserable.

"I am sick of it," Jay said. "We helped him when he lost his job and had his little family move in with us. We were happy to do it. But do you think he appreciated it? Absolutely not! He was nasty to Helen, and now that he is back on his feet, he hardly gives us the time of day, except when he needs something.

"Helen feels used, but she excuses him because she thinks somewhere along the line, she made mistakes raising the kids. A good cry and she's out there putting herself in the same situation.

"Not me. Paul is spoiled and inconsiderate. I am not going to forgive or forget. I can't trust him. He'd better not come asking me for a thing. If he does, I am going to tell him exactly what I think of him. If he doesn't ever talk to me again, so be it."

Wounded Egos

They won't admit it, but if you listen carefully to what some fathers have to say about being sidelined, you notice signs of wounded egos. This was not as much in play with mothers.

Bewildered and feeling put down, Fred explained, "My kids are domineering and pompous and act superior. My son even told me what I should or should not talk to his rich in-laws about. I am a professional man with a good education. They never ask for my opinion. When I do speak up, I sense they dismiss what I have to say. It's like they tolerate me. That's all."

In a separate interview, Fred's wife, a clinical social worker, said he feels diminished by his children's behavior.

"Our children shake up his self-image and confidence. It definitely impacts his ego," she said.

Feeling Disrespected

When responding to the question "how do your adult children treat you?" the most common negative answer was "without respect." Fathers, however, were offended by this behavior more than mothers.

"If they loved us, they would show respect with a capital *R*," Kenneth said. "If you love someone, you respect them."

When asked how his adult children could show respect and love, Kenneth responded like this:

"They could take time to visit us. They could talk nicely to us rather than respond with such a high and mighty attitude. They can be absolutely nasty.

"They don't have any appreciation for everything we did for them. They had the very best education.

"They wouldn't allow their husbands to be disrespectful. It is obvious our son-in-law merely stomachs us and doesn't especially like having us around. It is very uncomfortable. He won't start a conversation and never asks about what we are doing in our own lives. There is no interest in us whatsoever.

"I feel cheated, if you want to know the truth. I see other parents being treated the way we treated ours, with respect and love."

Getting worked up just talking about the situation, Kenneth seethed with anger. He wouldn't admit to being hurt, although it was obvious.

"I don't want to talk about it anymore. They aggravate me so much, I don't care if I go there ever again. I would rather stay home. Let my wife go. She will take anything just to see our grandchildren.

"I am not going to let these kids get the better of me," Kenneth concluded. But it is obvious they had.

Feeling loved is a terrific antidote to small infractions of seeming disrespect or dismissal. Perhaps Kenneth is feeling more unloved than disrespected. Knowing you are loved certainly lessens the sting of sidelining. It did for Janet.

"My daughter criticizes me," Janet noted, "but also treats me with love and care. I feel her love even when she rolls her eyes at me. Her love makes it easy for both of us to overlook a lot of things."

Stewing versus Venting

Women do both. They stew and vent to friends. Furthermore, moms seek professional counseling to deal with the pangs of being sidelined more often than dads do.

Men, on the other hand, don't want to address sidelining. If and when they do, it is most likely only with their spouse unless they are so frustrated that they talk to a friend whom they assume has similar issues. Otherwise, they stew silently or store the grievance in the back of their minds, acting as if they have been unaffected by their children's behavior.

This drives mothers crazy!

"My husband doesn't support me at all. He tells me to just leave it alone whenever I become upset with our daughter's husband. How can I leave it alone? He makes me feel as welcome as an ax-murderer."

It was obvious at a dinner that resulted in a venting session accompanying dessert that my friend's husband, Tom, was slightly amused by her rendition of their latest trip to visit their son.

"I was told I did a better job this time," my friend said, referring to her son's critique of her visit. "He said he could see that I was trying really hard, meaning I didn't do as much wrong as Jack normally thinks I do. Of course he thought that. I kept quiet the entire four days we were there and did exactly as I was told. I never voiced my opinion once or did anything I feared he or his wife might disapprove of. Before I suggested an activity with my grandsons, I asked for approval from Jack, who then discussed it with his wife and who then reported back to me whether it was okay or not. Did I have a good time? What do you think? No!

"Tom tells me I am too sensitive. But it doesn't feel good. I cry about it and try to put it away in my mind. It's less complicated that way."

Fortunately the rich, chocolate dessert and the opportunity to vent appeared to soothe my upset friend.

Victimhood

Everyone falls into the trap of feeling like a victim at some time or other. Don't get defensive here! No one is faulting you for acting like a victim. Victimhood is a natural human feeling. **But it is one that impedes your happiness and clouds your ability to evaluate your relationships.**

It is human nature for us to want to blame others, Pat explains. You can blame that on your ego. Your ego loves to be the victim. If we feel sorry for ourselves, it makes the other person bad, and we can be the good guy.

Some people get stuck in the victim mode and don't recognize that they:

A. Unconsciously don't want to be happy
B. Actually choose to be victims
C. Thrive on problems
D. Set themselves up for disappointment
E. Repeat the pattern in A through D over and over again
F. Haven't found a way to put their egos in check

A Case in Point

Not much feels right in Sonia's life. This mother of four sounded like a quintessential victim, feeling taken for granted and mistreated. A litany of complaints flowed out of her mouth. Only her fourth child, she noted, said sweet things to her.

"My daughter is uncommunicative with me. She excludes me and does what she wants.

"On Mother's Day, I felt abused by my son. I bought tickets to a play for all of the children and their significant others and then invited them for dinner afterward. It was a play I really had wanted to see and thought they would all enjoy it. My son and his fiancée ran in just as the curtain was going up and left immediately after the curtain went down. At intermission, they handed me a computer-generated card that surely was an afterthought.

"I spent Saturday at my middle son's home planting a garden for him. Did he thank me? No. Instead, he called me that night after having been with his sister, who told him I wasn't crazy about his girlfriend, and yelled at me, saying 'I hate you. We all hate you.'

"I couldn't believe it. My children used to make my life fulfilling. We used to share everything. I think I was an excellent but naïve mother. My husband was never around. I practically raised them on my own. Now they are aloof. They come over only to drop their dogs off if they are going out of town or stop for food. They have a drink while I am slaving away cooking. No one thinks to help me.

"My third son has a girlfriend. Her mother has cancer. They are so thoughtful and kind to her. Sometimes I think to myself that I wish I had cancer and were dying. Maybe they would appreciate me then."

Testing and Evaluating Your Responses

Step One—Testing

To take this test and make it count requires giving honest answers. Answer yes or no to each statement as it applies to how you feel. Check the appropriate column.

Statement:	**Yes**	**No**

1. If it weren't for my son/daughter, I would be just fine.
2. I feel sorry for myself.
3. My feelings get hurt a lot.
4. My misery is not really my fault.
5. I blame others for my problems.
6. I wonder why so many bad things happen to just me.
7. Events in my childhood still affect me.
8. I think I am owed certain things.
9. I deserve better than this.
10. I expect others to be aware of my feelings and make me feel good.

Step Two—Evaluating

The above ten statements are representative of how we think and feel in our victim mode.

If you put a yes by even one of these ten statements, you need to recognize that this is your victim mode talking, not your healthy self.

If you answered yes more than three times, you are probably stuck in the victim mode to some degree and are attempting to justify it.

Four or more positive responses means you are likely wallowing in the abyss and need to learn how to climb out of the black hole, or you will continue to be a very unhappy victim.

Step Three—Accepting the Implications

The following conclusions can be made at this point:

1) What should be clear from this introductory discussion of victimhood is that for the sake of your own happiness, your thinking may need an overhaul.

2) There is no way you can think clearly and without bias when your victimization script is in control.

3) Never allowing yourself to be the bad guy doesn't give you room to accept being wrong. That means no one else can be right.
4) Victims don't take responsibility for their own behavior, which is a recipe for misery.

Step Four—Altering Your Mind-Set

Fortunately, victimhood need not be a terminal or irreversible condition. No one has to remain a victim. However, only you can turn your mind-set around. As you continue to read through the chapters, you will be given tools to move past your victim mentality. There is no way to get over being sidelined until you legitimately shed this label.

Not Everyone Reacts to Sidelining

Here is where you get to meet the lucky parents who feel they have never been sidelined or who, more accurately, chose not to be affected by it. They are a very rare species.

Personality traits play a major role in how individuals react to sidelining. Parents who naturally have no issue with sidelining, or at the least, calmly overlook it, are generally easygoing, primarily accepting, and unlikely to get their feathers ruffled.

Darlene is a wonderful example. She and George have been married over twenty years. It is a second marriage for both of them. They each came to the altar with children whom they jointly participated in raising and claim an emotional investment in and attachment to. When asked about sidelining, Darlene said she got it, but it simply wasn't something she would react to.

"I have a very accommodating personality and easygoing, positive temperament," she said. "I came from a very accepting family. I don't hold on to grievances, and my expectations of people are low. Then I don't get disappointed."

On the other hand she said, "My husband does react and tries to get me aggravated, but he can't.

"It was the first Christmas after his daughter got married. We see her all the time. She lives very close. Anyway, her in-laws were coming in from out of town for the holiday. She didn't invite her father and me to Christmas dinner. I really feel I could have called her up and said we wanted to come. But I know she was nervous and wanted everything to be perfect. I didn't want to add to her pressure so was perfectly content inviting friends over instead.

"Yes, her father was miffed! The latest source of his aggravation is her habit of dropping by for only ten minutes with the baby. George isn't happy about that. He wants more."

On the other hand, Darlene is more willing to accommodate her children.

"My kids rarely come to town. Sure, I would love my daughter and grand-children to come visit us, but it's hard to travel with the kids. I am fortunate I can get on a plane and see them when I want to or if my daughter needs me. Whatever works is fine with me."

Admittedly, Darlene, a bright, educated, and retired lawyer, reacts the same way to her husband. She has no problem easily accommodating her schedule to fit her husband's plans, whether for dinner or an extended vacation, and she is happy to do it. She is content sitting back and enjoys whatever she is doing at the moment.

Darlene is a healthy, satisfied, and easygoing woman! Don't confuse Darlene's acceptance with being a wimp or a victim. She is choosing love and acceptance when confronted with behavior that her husband would find upsetting.

What's Next?

It shouldn't be difficult to conclude that sidelining is damaging to both adult offspring and their parents. Why has this important relationship spun so much discomfort and disappointment at this point in time?

The fascinating evolution of sidelining is uncovered in chapter 3. The causes are multiple. You will undoubtedly be surprised by some of our discoveries.

CHAPTER 3

How Did We Get Here?

W hy we find ourselves stuck in difficult relationships with our adult children today is an interesting and complicated story.
It is worthwhile to shine a spotlight on the atmosphere in which these young men and women were raised. Collective tendencies attributed to those now in their mid-twenties to late forties were influenced by the prevailing ideas and attitudes during this expanded time period.

Constructing and setting this stage is critical to tracing the development of sidelining and provides the necessary background upon which we should view our adult children today. How individual personalities and unique situations affect the syndrome is the focus of Part II.

Parenting within the Tone of the Era

There has never been a generation of parents that got it all right. It is impossible to be a perfect parent! No regrets or recriminations please. You tried and thoughtfully did what you assumed was best for your child in an era preoccupied with self-esteem issues and the pursuit of individual happiness and success.

Promoting High Self-Esteem and Unexpected Narcissism

Remember the mantra of parents from the late sixties onward, "Above all else we must nurture high self-esteem in our children"? The point of working on raising your children's self-esteem was to assure they would become healthy, wealthy, wise, and happy.

In the early 1970s, low self-esteem was viewed as the root cause of failure and human suffering. The antidote was love and self-acceptance. Moms and dads jumped on the bandwagon, heaping sound and empty praise on their children. By the 1980s, self-esteem was thought potent enough to be able to cure major social problems.

The popularization of enhancing individual self-esteem has been credited in large part to Nathaniel Branden, psychologist and author of *The Psychology of Self-Esteem*. Branden, married four times without having children, was a longtime lover of Ayn Rand and often credited with being "the father of the self-esteem movement."

Ironically, the mega-doses of medicine contrived to build self-esteem promoted a false sense of reality, contributed to self-centered adulation, and bred a generation of narcissists who feel entitled, are self-centered, and require admiration.

Well, who knew!

Psychologists Jean M. Twenge, PhD, and W. Keith Campbell, PhD, authors of *The Narcissism Epidemic*, trace the rise of the self-esteem trend in the seventies with its inherent focus on self as one of the social factors that exacerbated an epidemic of narcissistic behavior. Twenge's other book published in 2007 investigates children raised in the seventies, eighties and nineties. The title, *Generation Me; Why Today's Young Americans Are More Confident, Assertive, Entitled—and More Miserable Than Ever Before*, is telling!

From Authoritative Parent to Pal

The gurus of childrearing at the time were pediatrician Dr. Benjamin Spock and child psychologist Dr. Hiam Ginott, author of *Parent and Child*. Spock first popularized the move from rigid, authoritative parenting and replaced it with something considered much more permissive at the time. Ginott pioneered ways to carefully listen to and address children with compassion and love.

The ironclad rule of parents "I am right; you are wrong" was out! Love and understanding were in. Boundary setting was loosened, and punishments were supposed to be compassionate, expressed by cautiously phrased words to avoid potentially damaging messages.

Pat believes there is no doubt that with the introduction of Spock's and Ginott's theories, we validated our children and helped them respect themselves. Unfortunately, we got hung up on trying to be reasonable. Although we listened to whatever our children had to say and valued their opinions, we found it hard to set limits or say no. We wanted our children to like us. We wanted them to view us as approachable, nice, friends, and equals. In the process, we lost control and may have given them permission to respect parents less.

Fix-It Moms

Is it any wonder that in this era of wanting to please children, making them feel good and engineering a path for them to become self-fulfilled adults, parents may have overdone it?

Fix-it moms, parents who thought it was their responsibility to make sure their children avoided feeling pain, went to humorous lengths to make sure their children were happy. One mother admitted trying to set up a sleepover on a Friday night for her first grader. When several mothers said their daughters were already busy, she was certain there was a party her child had not been invited to. In order to head off any feelings of misery or exclusion that might impinge on her little girl's happiness, this mom didn't rest until she called every child she knew and found one who could spend the night. It didn't matter that she had to drive to the other side of town to pick up this child during a snowstorm. Later she learned that "the party" was a figment of her own tormented imagination.

The queen of fix-it moms recanted a simple incident that speaks volumes: "I can still see my then seven-year-old daughter coming down the steps in our home. All I did was look up at her. I hadn't spoken a word, and she said, 'Mom I swear I am happy!'"

Kids, the Center of Our Universe

The world in large part revolved around these children. To maximize their growth, parents indulged them with opportunities and experiences, sometimes at the cost of their own financial wellbeing. Before this research began, I (Rosanne) remember speaking to a single, professional mother who held two jobs and moved into a small one-room apartment to save money during the years her son was in college so that he didn't have to spend time working and could focus on his studies.

Among the more affluent sectors of society, children were indulged in other ways. They attended sports camps to prepare for team tryouts, traveled abroad to expand their horizons, and attended prestigious summer school sessions to boost their competitive edge and improve their chances of getting into the college of their choice. Anything and everything was done to ensure success and augment their carefully crafted confidence.

Moms are still anguishing over their children even after they reach adulthood. A certain amount of worry is normal and beneficial. But **we are still a generation way too affected by our kids!**

"Their unhappiness makes me unhappy," says Andrea, referencing her thirty-eight-year-old daughter and forty-five-year-old son. She isn't alone. Our questionnaires consistently validated that unhappy children make for unhappy parents.

Zoey admits that she suffers terribly when her kids are unhappy. That's what happened when one of her married kids had an affair. "I was miserable. My daughter was upset with herself, and her husband was so upset. I wanted their life to get back on track so much. I thought they would all be unhappy forever and that a divorce would affect my grandchildren. I wouldn't have been able to stand it! I was so grateful when they worked it out."

Our Adult Children as Child-Centered Hyper-Parents

Trends, theories, and practices don't change quickly. They either fizzle out slowly, maintain a status quo, or mutate. In our opinion, there seems to be ample evidence that the atmosphere in which our adult children are parenting is often a steroidal mutation of all we described already at play in their youth.

Our adult children are caught in a world of child-centered families and hyper-parenting. Child-centered parents put their kids first, use most of their personal and financial resources for the benefit of their offspring, and look for ways to be more effective parents. There are at least a hundred parenting books on Amazon.com, grocery store racks full of childrearing articles, and abundant community courses on parenting.

With so much to consider and at stake in raising children, is it any surprise that these parents have sometimes become comically vigilant and uncompromising micromanagers of the minutest aspects of their offspring's life? Early childhood allergies, protective parenting, and making mountains out of molehills are in. Common sense or risk taking is out. Nap times to bath times are sacred hours, unapproved foods are off limits, and any lag or difference in development is cause for immediate action.

To illustrate the latter point, Alvin Rosenfeld, MD, New York psychiatrist and author of *The Over-Scheduled Child*, used an amusing story. The mother of a five-year-old girl was told that her daughter had a "pencil-holding" deficiency and needed a tutor to correct it. Rosenfeld approved of the mother's wisdom in ignoring the issue. Dr. Rosenfeld reported that the young woman is now succeeding in college and holding her pencil in exactly the same fashion.

No wonder this milieu has produced what Rosenfeld calls hyper-parents. He describes them as moms and dads who run their sleep-deprived high school students to endless enrichment or sports activities and a plethora of tutors, all in order to raise the perfect child who can qualify for the college of his or her dreams. While hyper-parents act with the best intentions, Rosenfeld says, they fail to realize they are sending their kids negative messages like "we are worried about your future" or "you aren't really as great as we say you are so you need more help."

Other professionals find reason to sound a note of caution when it comes to child-centered parenting: it can create self-entitled monsters who feel significant pressure to fulfill the emotional needs of the parents who are overly focused and sacrifice too much for them.

How Hyper-Parenting Affects the Grandparent Generation

The point of this introduction to child-centered hyper-parenting families is not to judge or demean. Rather the purpose is to illuminate the following:

- Why our adult kids are so busy and preoccupied
- How all parents fall prey to influences permeating the atmosphere
- How our adult children are often more invested in and obsessive about their kids than we were
- How the values have shifted so that grandma and grandpa are second or third fiddle to nearly everything else
- Why parents may be overly defensive, be exceptionally protective, and suffer more angst than previous generations

Our Adult Children under the Microscope

A look at the collective will give you insight into your own adult child and his or her generation. Furthermore, it lets you know exactly where your family member is coming from and, in part, why your kids respond to you in the ways they do.

Generational Differences in Place Today

Take these generational differences as facts. Do not react to them emotionally, although you will want to. Many will be offensive and do not represent your values. They are, nonetheless, prevailing attitudes in place today. Repeated and reinforced by the multitudes of our adult children, some or all are bound to seriously color your relationship.

Multiple sources concur with the following:

1) Roles are less prescribed today
2) There is a greater sense of freedom and exposure
3) The extended family is unraveling

4) Nuclear-style families of all configurations are in

5) There is more focus on the individual

6) Self-centeredness is considered a good thing

7) There is greater acceptance of differences

8) Substance abuse is relatively common

9) Fewer adult children live in the same cities as their parents

10) Technology has affected and altered the way we communicate with each other

Characteristics of the Generation

Whether you call them Generation X, the Millennials, the Me Generation, or any other name, the following characteristics are attributed by the mass media to the age group of the adult kids in our study:

- Relatively well educated
- Individualistic
- Independent
- Resourceful
- Technologically savvy
- Work to live
- Play hard
- Underemployed
- Self-centered
- Entitled
- Blaming
- Frequently anxious, depressed, and substance dependent

How Parents Describe the Generation

The following represents the consensus of opinion among participants in our study in reference to the entire generation, not necessarily their own children. Supportive data was found in a variety of popular-based articles.

When asked, "How would you describe your adult children's generation?" parents replied with the following adjectives:

- Spoiled
- Entitled
- Too busy
- Demanding
- Self-absorbed
- Inflexible
- Lacking empathy
- Defensive

Differences in Adult Child–Parent Relationships

Contemporary family relationships seem significantly different from their parents' generation. Pat maintains this generation of adult children:

1. Demand that parents earn their respect and love
2. Don't work at their relationships with their parents
3. Believe parents will always be there
4. Use their children as pawns to punish or reward grandma and grandpa

Factors That Exacerbate the Sidelining Phenomenon

Social attitudes, adult children's perspective, and parents' expectations collide under the cloud of contemporary life, exacerbating the onset of sidelining. There are a number of changes, particularly within the family, that disrupt the adult child–parent relationship. We will examine those first and then proceed to identify other forces at play.

Diminishing Family Loyalty and Differing Priorities

From the parents' point of view, there isn't any doubt that family loyalty has fallen short of late. But remember, loyalty is a very subjective topic and a matter of perception and interpretation. However, it is fair to say that adult children's sense of allegiance to their extended family is challenged by priorities, time constraints, marriage, hyper-parenting, and greater emotional or physical separation.

In the ultra-busy world of working and playing hard, accompanied with toting young kids from one activity to another, parents have lots of competition for their adult children's time and attention.

I was sitting in a pedicure chair with two thirty-something women on each side of me. It was two days before Christmas. They exchanged greetings and asked one another about holiday plans with their children.

"We are going to stay home, veg out, then drive to my in-laws the day after Christmas," the first woman said.

Her friend replied, "Oh, that sounds wonderful! We have to be at my parents'. That's what happens when you have relatives in town."

Intrigued by their answers, I struck up a conversation with the young woman heading out of town and asked how she and her husband determined which set of parents they would share the post-holiday with. She explained that they had already spent Thanksgiving with her folks, who live six hours south of them and come twice a year to see her. In addition, she and her family go to their home generally another two times a year. So going to her in-laws worked out "especially well."

Picking up on the "especially" part, I had to ask "How so?"

Her husband's parents had wanted to visit in the fall, but it wasn't a good time for her husband, so she had to tell them not to come.

"It's the busiest time of the year for my husband," she said. "It would have been too hard."

Although I had no way of speaking to her in-laws, a great many other parents would have perceived this type of attitude as lack of loyalty based upon a profound sense of their children's misplaced priorities, loss of closeness, an absence of allegiance, ungratefulness, and unfeeling.

Here are three more examples given in our interviews that further illustrate what most of the parents we spoke with describe as a lack of family loyalty. The action is always the same—adult kids choose someone or something over time with parents.

Example A

"My kids would rather spend holidays, Sunday evenings, or vacations with their friends," Margaret began. "I invite them for dinner all the time. Rarely do they accept. I think the reality of them choosing their friends over their family is more painful because they live in town near us. I see my grandsons once a month and have lunch with my son every now and then. I feel so excluded. I don't get it."

Example B

Gary, well into his eighties, matter-of-factly states that he certainly isn't a priority in his youngest son's life. "He was a late-in-life child and spoiled. He will rent a private plane to go to a golf tournament a thousand miles away, but when it comes to flying out to see me, he says he is too busy. And when he does plan to visit, I never know if he will show. His track record isn't very good. Usually a meeting comes up that he says he can't miss. It's his life. What am I going to do?"

Example C

Aaron and Lela have two children. They come from a culture where family is of the highest priority. A sense of duty and love toward family members is readily apparent to any observer. Upon retirement, Aaron and Lela decided to relocate closer to their oldest son. A prerequisite in the purchase of a new home was a lovely suite for Lela's mother.

When the first religious holiday approached a few weeks after their move, Aaron and Lela had the shock of their lives. They assumed the holiday would be spent in the company of their son. It never occurred to them that their daughter-in-law's family, who shares their cultural background, would exclude them. Not wanting to cause trouble, they said nothing, but their sadness was profound. They were highly insulted by their daughter-in-law's family but equally dismayed that their bright, well-educated son made no attempt to rectify the situation. Instead of wallowing in loneliness, they flew back to the city in which they had lived and shared the holiday with other relatives.

Separation with a Capital *S*
The emotional separation of this generation from their parents is greater than we have previously witnessed. The adult children Pat has encountered are more able to say good-bye without a sense of loss when they no longer have a need for mom and dad. These offspring seem more insular, more self-centered, and less empathetic.

The normal parent-child separation is generally defined as the time when a mature child assumes responsibility for his or her own life. This separation develops gradually after the turbulent teens. The following seem to characterize the contemporary emotional separation now between parent and adult children:

- More tension
- The absence of comfortable or relaxed interaction
- A focus on the exclusivity of nuclear family life with less desire to include parents unless they are doing something for the adult children
- The inability of adult children to recognize their parents as individuals with lives and emotions of their own

Marriage Alters the Parental Relationship
Marriage diminishes the position of moms and dads in their adult children's lives. The behavior exhibited by newly married couples toward their parents may feel like sidelining when:

1) Mom and dad are relegated to the backseat in light of their adult child's new alliance
2) The less dominant individual in the marriage may find it difficult to ask his or her partner to shape up and treat his or her parents with more kindness and respect
3) One partner does not share the desire to be invested with the extended family

Bonding, an Act of Exclusion and Separation

It is fair to conjecture that emotional separation is not entirely linked to adult children living in different locales than their parents but perhaps to the way coupled life is approached today. Indeed, much of what is inherent in the popularization of "family bonding" excludes the extended family and encourages emotional and physical separation.

At its core, bonding is a natural process that is now accompanied by "how-to" manuals on family activities for parents and children of all ages, just one more thing on the "to-do" list for adult children raising their own brood. Granted, there is a plethora of advice on how grandparents can bond with grandchildren, but adult kids bonding with their parents is ignored almost entirely in popular self-help literature.

Here is what the bonding now looks like.

Example A

Julie, a devoted only child, lived in Bermuda, thousands of miles from her widowed mother. She, her husband, and toddler sons made the trip to visit her mother for less than a week. Within that time period, Julie made it clear to her mother that she was not invited to join them on an outing to the zoo. They needed family time alone, she explained.

Example B

My own daughter asked me to stay at a hotel, not in her home, when she came from the hospital with her first child, even though my job was to help with the baby and the household. I was told, "We need time by ourselves to bond."

The Super Influential Son- or Daughter-in-Law

We could fill this chapter with stories of the villainous sons- or daughters-in-law, particularly the latter. Instead, we will settle for a few. Previous pages have been peppered with examples. How to deal with these outlaw children will be detailed in Part III.

Sons- and daughters-in-law can wreak havoc in a family. In our investigation, their spouses' parents considered them the primary instigators of sidelining who inflicted the greatest damage and provoked the largest misunderstandings.

The most extreme example of mothers and daughters-in-law conflicts we came across was a mom whose interactions were limited solely to her married son. His wife refused to acknowledge the existence of her husband's family.

Phyllis, on the other hand, might have liked to limit her relationship to her son void of his wife, but she knew she would be the one left out in the cold.

"I didn't want to cross my daughters-in-law," Phyllis explained. "However, there is one whose behavior makes me cringe. She bullies my son and their children. But I have never said anything to her or him. I have never opened up, but I have walked out. After I walked out once, I didn't hear from my child for six months. Yes, it hurts right in your heart. But she can never exclude me from my son. I would never let anyone stand between my children and me no matter how horrible that person is.

"You just smile and keep on going as if everything is all right. I am older now and at a stage where I don't have to depend on my children to see my grandchildren. I have lived long enough to work around it. I am just at a stage in my life where I don't have to be with certain people who change my day."

Unresolved Issues with Divorce

According to published statistics, at the time the adult children in our study were growing up, the US divorce rate soared, almost doubling from 1965 to 1980.

If you opted for personal happiness through divorce, you may accidentally have opened up another realm of adversities that still affect your adult child–parent relationship today.

Children of divorce are often conflicted over issues of parental loyalty, particularly where there is the perception that one parent was responsible for the family breakup.

Example #1

Rachel was ten years old when her mother and father divorced.

"My mom never talked badly about my father and tried to keep all the stuff that was going on out of eyesight. She wanted me to feel it was okay for him to be there for me if I wanted. When I was eleven, she remarried. My relationship with my mother is a ten, with my stepfather an eight, and a zero with my real father. I haven't spoken to him in ten years. Now that I am older and looking back, I have great respect for what mom did by divorcing him. He was an alcoholic and an abuser, but she didn't want to color my opinion of him. My mother has the biggest heart of anyone I've ever known. We have a unique relationship, closer than most."

Example #2

CiCi, in her late thirties, has held on to her anger since her father left her mother years ago. Charlie cannot understand why his daughter is always angry with him. He thinks her beef isn't legitimate. CiCi, who Charlie feels has always taken her mother's side, has asked him for money more than once—not for her but for her terminally ill mother. It seems she is now broke. But Charlie refused to help, which created a new round of ill will. CiCi has remained steadfast on her mother's side.

Example #3

There are many parents who haven't worked through the pain of divorce and often don't realize they have the "I have been wronged" mentality. There is no reason to hold on to these grievances; they aren't good for you. The kids get caught in the middle, no matter what age they are, and the parents raise the risk for serious, hurtful sidelining.

This very well could have been a contributing factor in Martha's case when she found herself sidelined in a majorly surprising and painful manner.

"It wasn't until my children were adults that I became the villain," Martha said. "I didn't want my kids to know certain things when they were younger. My husband treated me very badly and left me for another woman. When my oldest son was getting married, he commented he didn't even know why we got divorced. That was more than ten years ago. So I wrote a letter to him and his brother explaining what had transpired.

"My oldest son didn't speak to his father for about a year. Then the boys decided, in consultation with each other, that they were going to overlook the past and were not going to take on the burden of my history. They wanted their father in their lives. They wanted him to be a grandfather to their children.

"I was angry, upset, and felt betrayed. I told them I couldn't believe they bought into their father's lies and bullshit. I had to be honest. I went to therapy on and off to try and get a hold on the bigger picture.

"My younger son is engaged, and my ex-husband will be a part of the wedding. Seeing him still has a physical effect on me. I can't stand to be around him. Fortunately, I rarely have to, and I stay away when he comes to see the grandkids. For the most part, my children know how I feel. It hasn't been an issue with my boys. Their father lives fifteen hundred miles from me, but his visits still create havoc.

"My ex happened to be coming to town for a few days to see the children and grandchildren when my younger son was going to be visiting as well. I was insistent that I wanted a few hours alone together with my son and grandchildren. It was apparent my daughter-in-law was annoyed with me. So I told my son to arrange it. I didn't see why my ex couldn't give up the kids for a few hours.

"The following week, I received a scathing note from my daughter-in-law, with whom I thought I shared a good relationship. I helped with the kids, took her to lunch, and stayed out of their way. Evidently, I wasn't as perfect as I thought I was. She told me I was selfish and created unnecessary trouble. Furthermore, she said she had never liked me!

"I was crushed. I left a message at my son's house that I wasn't available for babysitting that week. I wanted to call and tell him what happened, but I didn't. I knew he and his wife were close, and in all honesty, there had to have been some discussion in the house. Whether or not he knew about the note, I am not sure. I prefer to believe he didn't. Otherwise, the idea that he didn't insist she apologize feels like a terrible betrayal by my own child. Could I possibly mean that little to him that he would condone his wife's written attack?

"I made excuses for weeks not to see them or the children—not that they tried to engage me. I felt like an unwelcome outsider. It took nearly a year of therapy to feel comfortable enough to carry on a normal relationship with either my son or daughter-in-law."

Money Matters

This is a hard one to quantify in dollars, cents, or statistics. Nonetheless, there is sufficient anecdotal evidence to indicate a strong connection between the adult child–parent's relationship and money. Let's be clear here, we are not talking about recent college grads who haven't been able to find a job and move home temporarily. Rather, the focus is on adult children who show no compunction asking for money, expecting financial assistance, or feeling entitled to their parents' resources.

Secondly, our observations were not limited to adult children whose parents sit in the upper 1 percent of the economic strata. **Taking advantage of mom's or dad's generosity is seen across the financial spectrum.**

The cases that follow demonstrate that despite the generosity of parents, adult children from all financial levels of society are perfectly willing to sideline their parents when money matters don't go their way.

Case #1

Samantha owns a residential and commercial cleaning business. She will work seven days a week if necessary to honor all of her contracts. Her daughter, an unmarried twenty-seven-year-old, lived with her unemployed boyfriend and their three-year-old son in a property Samantha owns. They were asked to pay

$300 in monthly rent, but at times failed to do so. Consequently, Samantha determined it was time her daughter got to work.

For several weeks, Samantha's daughter worked alongside her, learning how to be fastidious and thorough enough to take over a few of her mother's clients, who pay more than $20 an hour. Within months, Samantha's daughter failed to fulfill her work obligations. Samantha asked her daughter to pay up her mounting debt. Trying to collect presented problems. Her daughter evidently saw no reason to comply. Rather she pouted, argued, and stomped out of the house like a mad child. Within months, she was pregnant again, expecting her mom to foot the bills and take care of her family.

Samantha's daughter had her mom pegged just right. There was no way Samantha could refuse to help provide her grandchildren with everything they needed.

Case #2

Robert moved into his parent's upper-middle class home, bringing his wife and child along when he was out of work for a few years. His wife's salary was not enough to enable them to live in a good school district like his parents did.

"I did it for my grandchild," Mary said. "It would have been okay, but my son is manipulative, defensive, argumentative, and disrespectful. He can really bring me down. After two years, he finally found a job and moved his family out. Last month, he called and wanted me to pay some of his bills. There was no way.

"He wasn't happy about it. Fortunately, he can't completely ignore me, because I am needed to pick up his child after school."

Money Speaks

"Money speaks" is a blunt and honest statement. It works in a multitude of ways and may affect the amount of time adult children spend with their parents.

Succinctly put by one multimillionaire dad, "The more toys you have at your house, the more often the kids come over."

In his case, it is a main house with a swimming pool and two vacation homes.

On the other side of the coin, a young surgeon just beginning his professional life told me, "Once I can afford to pay for our vacations, we won't have to go with my parents or my wife's."

The truth is, we did find that parents become more expendable when adult kids don't need their financial resources or help. Money does matter! There is no doubt that it is a factor that can influence adult child–parent relationships, interaction, and potential sidelining.

Substance Abuse and Poor Mental Health Issues, Serious Family Busters

Substance abuse and problems with mental health are prominent among the cohort of adult children we are focused upon. In fact, studies show the following:

1) Twenty-six-to-forty-nine-year-olds have more substance abuse and emotional problems than in the past.

2) Prescription drug abuse is five times more prevalent than in 1990, according to the State Department of Health and Human Services.

3) Mental health issues have increased over 6 percent for adults between the ages of twenty-one and forty-nine.

Drugs and alcohol are family destroyers and causes of extreme sidelining. These substances take precedence over everything else and become primary to the user.

A concern Pat notes is that parents of adult children are naïve when it comes to detecting drug and alcohol abuse and are afraid to talk to their adult kids about it for fear of being further alienated. Moms and dads don't readily recognize the signs of substance abuse and don't question why their sons or daughters are distant, unhappy, asking for money, and unable to settle down. There is so much deceit generated by the user that often families know something is terribly wrong but cannot understand why this individual has become uncaring, self-centered, nonfunctioning, unloving, disrespectful, difficult, and illusive.

The Blame Game Generation

There is another sidelining factor, prevalent enough among our spectrum of adult children, to deserve its own extensive discussion. Sometimes the "blame game" takes ridiculously convoluted formats that defy our imagination. So let's begin this subject with a bit of levity. I didn't make this one up, nor did the mother who told me about it.

"I have two daughters in their forties. The older one had a dream in which she and her sister became pregnant by the same man. They didn't get mad at each other or their cheating lover. Instead they blamed me. My daughter was laughing when she told me about the dream. I didn't think it was so humorous."

Of course, this mother didn't think it was funny. She had been blamed too many times before. But her daughter's dream does illustrate just about how absurd and outrageous the blame game can be.

How the Blame Game Is Played

The fact is when adult kids grow up, leave a child-centered protective environment, and find life in the real world more difficult than they are equipped to handle, they have to find someone to blame for their lack of success. Parents were so invested in their children's lives and took such complete responsibility for their upbringing that they actually opened the door for blaming them.

If your adult children don't get along with you, it's your fault—not theirs! If adult children aren't happy, it's your fault—not theirs. If adult children don't have ample self-esteem, it's your fault—not theirs! If adult children can't get a job, it's your fault—not theirs! If adult children don't have a satisfying, loving partnership, it's your fault—not theirs! Somehow, they believe their parents should have given them even more tools to promote a good relationship, grow their self-esteem, or find success in the workplace.

Projecting blame onto someone else has a self-serving bias; it protects self-esteem, alleviates responsibility, and confirms one's sense of rightness. Ultimately, however, blame makes the blamers miserable.

Holding on to blame isn't something our adult children do in a vacuum. It is very much a part of the milieu in which they relate to others. We can safely say that "blaming" is currently institutionalized behavior. If kids aren't doing well in school today, it's the teacher's fault. If adults aren't promoted at work, it's because their superiors don't like them. If people are overweight, it's because fattening fast food is too available.

What concerns us is that the blame game is disastrous for a good relationship with your adult children.

Halting the Blame Game

Blaming parents for anything or everything will never come to a stop until adult children:

1) Take personal responsibility for who they are
2) Accept parents as individuals with feelings and imperfections

Without embracing these conditions, there is no way to give up a grudge and move the relationship in a more positive direction.

Blamers and Non-Blamers

It is easier for blamers not to take any responsibility for the difficulties in a relationship. If they do, they have to grow up, admit they aren't always right, and possibly alter their behavior to make things better.

Non-blamers accept their parents, faults and all. They can forgive and forget what it was they might have blamed them for before they grew up and took responsibility for themselves.

A Close-up of a Blamer

Tara's parents came for a month to help after she delivered her third child. Instead of being grateful, the time together confirmed her opinion that the problems she had with her parents were entirely their fault.

"They are too rigid. They only see things their way, and they always have," Tara began. "I had to go to the private school they picked out and make friends with kids within certain circles. They were very old fashioned. I was very lonely and would sneak out of the house to see my friends. A few times, I thought maybe I was pregnant. I couldn't go to them; I went to my nanny. Whatever I did was not good enough. I know I hold on a lot to the past and have old grudges, but I never felt loved. It still doesn't feel like a comfortable, loving relationship.

"If we get into an argument, my mother tells me I am a very bitter person. I know they see me as disrespectful. I don't feel they are respecting me. Recently, my father and I had a fight on the phone. He hung up. If I don't talk to him for months, it is fine. It won't bother me. I can just walk away."

A Close-up of a Non-blamer

Meet Alex, an accepting and nonjudgmental thirty-year-old with an unusual—okay, *whacky*—no-frills family background. His life started off differently from the norm right from the get-go. He was given the full name (first, middle, and last) of an uncle whom his father admired and loved. Alex's last name was different from his mother's, father's, and sisters'. He said living with his parents—a genius dad who possessed no social skills and a nonconformist, ultra-religious mom who out of necessity struggled as the breadwinner—was like sharing a home with an aunt and an uncle.

Admittedly, Alex said, he was always outside of the mainstream community in which they lived and got into trouble when he was young. He doesn't blame his parents for any of his adolescent problems. Nor does he blame them now.

"It's who they are. Why blame them?" Alex said, wishing his upbringing could have been different but resigned to the childhood he had.

Rather than carry a grudge, Alex is accommodating. Despite his disappointment that his mother would not attend the ceremony in which he married a woman from a different ethnic and religious background, he refuses to hold it against her. He and his wife visit regularly but stay at a friend's house where they feel more comfortable.

Alex's parents are two lucky people. And Alex most definitely has no signs or symptoms of a blamer!

What's Next?

You should have a good idea now how sidelining develops and how it has surfaced into a syndrome of epidemic proportions. If you comprehend that and add it to your clear image of the sidelining syndrome and how it affects parents of adult children, you are properly prepared to begin examining this behavior in a more personal way. Doing so, however, won't be effective in finding the happiness you deserve unless you approach the remainder of the information in the book with an open mind.

Part II: Confronting Sidelining with an Open Mind

B eginning to come to terms with sidelining means considering the behavior from all points of view. To accomplish this, we will give adult kids a chance to speak and uncover who is most likely to sideline and be sidelined. You will be provided as well with stepping-stones and enlightening new concepts that hold the key to more objectively evaluating your adult child–parent relationship, the state of your family, and your emotional status.

As you read the following pages, you might or might not feel exonerated from blame; at other moments, you will recognize that your pain comes from within yourself; and you may realize that changing your child's behavior toward you is not a possibility.

Most importantly, you will be well on your way to stake a claim over your emotions, actions, thoughts, and feelings. **Taking responsibility for how you feel will free you from the turmoil you have been experiencing, put you in a happier place, and enable you to claim a healthier future.**

Each and every word in Part II is meant to prepare you to take the utmost advantage of the wisdom, exercises, and directives that will be brought to you in Part III. Therefore, consider all of the knowledge presented in these chapters carefully and thoughtfully. You are building the foundation for a better life that will finally place you in control and liberate you from the sting of sidelining

CHAPTER 4

Cutting the Kids Some Slack

There is value in stepping back and listening to what adult children have to say. You may decide there is some truth in what they have put forth or that they are overly sensitive, just don't get it, or are unwilling to cut parents any slack. There is most likely a shred of truth in all of these possibilities. But most importantly, this chapter is written to help you gain a better perspective on what's influencing your adult children's sidelining.

No doubt the poster kids we introduce you to will make you salivate with envy. However, these sons and daughters are presented to help you determine whether or not your offspring have the desire, potential, or ability to improve their relationships with you.

What Our Adult Kids Think of Us

Compatible family members, as well as those with obvious grievances, have adult kids who voice the same highly subjective complaints about parents. Among those polled in our sample, parents were deemed as follows:

- Critical
- Judgmental
- Opinionated
- Free with advice (unsolicited or otherwise)
- Demanding

- Controlling
- Intrusive

Do These Characteristics Contribute to Sidelining?

In general, the answer is yes. However, whether or not these behaviors encourage sidelining in your adult children is determined by how they feel affected:

- If interpreted as merely annoying behaviors, the easier they are to ignore and forgive and forget
- If, on the other hand, they are received as reprimands or insults, it is more likely that they will produce feelings of guilt, anger, and inadequacy that frequently encourage the onset of sidelining

What Do Your Adult Kids Think of You?

List a few of the labels you might be assigned by your adult offspring:

1) _____

2) _____

3) _____

4) _____

List some of your behaviors that seem to bring on the sidelining:

1) _____

2) _____

3) _____

4) _____

Do You Deserve to Be Sidelined?

You probably aren't able to answer that question accurately yet. However, your responses to the questions above will provide an initial glimmer of insight as to what that answer might be.

Roberta, on the other hand, gave a resounding yes. Her story is not told to insinuate that many of us deserve to be sidelined. Rather, the point is to illustrate that sometimes, we are not fully aware of our own behavior.

For seven years, Roberta complained bitterly that she was rarely invited over to her son and daughter-in-law's home, infrequently granted time with her grandchildren, and refused assistance when her son's stepfather went through numerous debilitating surgeries. Roberta's relationship with her son was on the brink of a total breakdown, and she blamed it entirely on her daughter-in-law.

"Larry was my only child. I guess I was pretty possessive, having raised him on my own. When he brought home my daughter-in-law for the first time, I instantly took a dislike to her and the way she spoke to my son. I never really gave her a chance. I was critical of her housekeeping, the way she was raising the children, and the fact that she kept Larry away from me. One day, it was like a bolt of lightning; I realized I had been acting like my mother-in-law, who had made me miserable. I was mortified. I didn't want to be like her.

"I went to see my daughter-in-law and apologized for everything I had done. She listened and was receptive to me. A few days later, she came over to see me and apologized for withholding Larry and the kids from me. Since then, we have developed a really nice relationship. I am sincerely grateful she could forgive me and allow me a second chance.

"I have my son back and am part of his family now. I can't believe how wonderful it feels."

The Mind-Set of Poster Kids

We have spotted adult children you would love to call your own. They have terrific relationships with their parents, whom they respect, appreciate, and include in their lives.

So what makes these kids different from the cadre of sideliners we have identified? Have they had perfect parents, or are they perfect kids? Of course, neither is the case. Rather, they miraculously and naturally do the following:

- Highly value the extended family
- Recognize the importance of harmonious family relationships
- Have partners who share their family vision
- Want parents in their lives
- Have good self-images
- Accept parents for who they are
- Appreciate what was and is done for them
- Do not have big, unresolved issues with their parents

Meet the Poster Children

What these adult kids have to say will warm your parental hearts. They aren't just saying what we want to hear. We have checked each of them out from all points of view and in many cases interviewed their parents as well. These adult kids have that magical combination that makes for good, warm and easy relationships—most of the time. As idyllic as these descriptions sound, these relationships aren't sustained at a top level 365 days a year. But they are about as good as it gets a majority of the time. We are human, after all!

In Sue's Words

"Before we married, we discussed our values and listed the things in life that are the most important to us. Our agreement about family first started there. We vowed to support the other in making sure that one another's in-laws were always treated with the respect and dignity that we chose for our own parents. They deserve that, no matter what the history or current circumstances. We both wanted to do this simply because they are our parents, and we love them. Life is short, and we wanted to make beautiful memories we can cherish and hold on to later.

"We respect our parents as individuals, who, like all other human beings, are not perfect. We are grateful for them having tried their best to parent us by doing everything they felt was right for us. We know as parents that it is hard. We are not perfect parents, so how could we hold on to anything from the past or even the present that we perceive as imperfect? We don't believe our parents should be held to an impossible standard. Nor do we want to be held to that standard by our parents or our children.

"We both feel that having parents and grandparents is a blessing. We do not take that for granted. We want our children to get to experience the beauty of having grandparents in their lives who love them so much and want to be with them.

"Our goal is to model the respect that we expect our children to show our parents and us. We believe in acts of kindness, and who better to give them to than family members—especially parents and grandparents?"

Perry and Amy's Conclusions

Perry is in his late forties, happily married, and devoted to his mother—he always has been. A handsome, athletic, well-established, confident, and successful lawyer-educated businessman, one would never imagine there was a problem in Perry's privileged, suburban childhood home.

"My father was an alcoholic and worked all the time. Mom was everything to us. Dad was never involved, but later, he was great with the grandkids. He was kind, but he never hugged or kissed you. I wanted and needed his acceptance. I had very low self-esteem growing up. I think he was proud of me. I had a good work ethic and worked at his company each summer after I turned thirteen.

"I appreciate what my parents sacrificed for me and wake up every day wanting to do the best I can for them."

When Perry's father was diagnosed with terminal cancer, he visited him daily and helped out as much as possible. Now that his mother is widowed, he stops on his way home from the office to check in on her. In a cracked, teary voice, Perry's mom expressed how much she missed his family when she went to Florida for the winter. Perry found cheap flights for the five of them to spend an upcoming long holiday weekend to cheer her up.

Perry's pretty wife, Amy, shares his commitment to all of their parents, whom she genuinely likes.

"Growing up, there weren't any real issues or conflicts in our home," Amy said. "I never realized how hard my father worked to provide for the family. I respect him for that today. There is nothing our parents could say or do that would change our minds about our families. We really sincerely have an open door at our house. My mom has a key and comes in whenever she wants like it's her own house. We wish Perry's mom would do it more. I never realized this is unusual. I never thought not to share my life with our parents. Family is the most important thing to both of us. I can't imagine how anyone could treat parents differently. We would both rather be with our parents than friends, but they would never make us choose."

Amy and Perry rated their relationships with their respective parents a ten. Not surprisingly, so did their parents.

Claire's Understanding

Thirty-five year old Claire is a daughter, a therapist, a wife, and a mother. Claire's parents divorced when she was two years old. Their separation did not create any problems for her, although she isn't as close to her father, who lives nearby.

"It's a work in progress. I see my dad but am not fully satisfied. I want more time together and more understanding between us.

"One of the biggest problems among my contemporaries is their unwillingness to stop dwelling on past conflicts and hurt. The kids need to make changes and have a desire to talk things through. It's time to get over it and be committed to working through these things.

"My mother and I have a great relationship because we are honest and direct in our communication and have an ability to see each other's perspective. There is no malice in what we say to each other. We are willing to have hard talks about hard moments without getting defensive. It's a way to build intimacy.

"I have a good understanding of my mother and love her dearly, even though her opinions are very strong and could cause conflict or arguments because I am more sensitive than she is and still sense myself wanting her approval. Recently, she delivered unsolicited advice on parenting in a way that I didn't like. She hurt my feelings. I e-mailed her and told her I didn't need her to say that again. There was no defensive reply.

"I can't think of anything that could come between me and my mother," Claire said. "There is nothing I don't want my mother to be involved in, but she doesn't have to be a part of everything. My top priority is family."

Poster Kids with Non-Poster Siblings

Most often, not every adult child in the same family turns out to be a poster child. If you have one, consider yourself lucky! And not all adult offspring within the same family are poster children to the same degree. The dynamics that contribute to the making of a poster child are more complicated than they appear to be.

For instance, consider these questions:

- Why are two adult children in a family poster perfect, while their siblings aren't?
- Why are some parents unable to recognize a poster child?
- Why might a problematic parent end up with poster children and a poster parent end up with a problematic adult child?

Easily Identifiable Differences among Siblings

Personality differences, formative experiences, and past or present perspectives make a huge impact on how adult siblings react and relate to their parents.

According to our research, non-poster kids who had a poster sibling tended to do the following:

- Be more self-centered and self-absorbed
- Engage more readily in the blame game
- Hang on to unresolved family issues
- Be less empathetic

- Have lower self-esteem
- Respond more argumentatively
- Be less open-minded
- Have more personal issues and stresses

Adult children who possess these factors are more difficult to please and easier to offend. People who are touchy generally have underlying, residual issues that haven't been forgiven or resolved. Mothers and fathers cannot beat themselves up over the past when they tried hard as parents to do the right thing. Nor should they take blame. Inborn characteristics, according to some professionals, account for approximately 50 percent of an individual's personality.

Parental Perceptions of Poster Kids

Let's face it. You may have an adult child in your life who is a lot closer to being a poster kid than you think. Perhaps the problem lies in your perceptions of your children.

In that case, ask yourself these questions:

- Am I expecting too much from my children?
- Am I unwilling to be compromising or open-minded?

Poster Kids with Difficult Parents

There is no denying that adult children may have flawed perceptions of their parents. But the kinds of behaviors attributed to the difficult parents we are talking about are blatant and constant.

For instance, difficult parents have no problem speaking their minds. These are just a few of their comments, but you will get the gist of it: "Your wife is getting fat." "I am more important than your spouse." "You could have included me in your family vacation." "I can't imagine what you see in your husband." "Your wife is so mean." "You don't know what you are doing." "You're a slob." "You wait on your husband too much." "You should have chosen a different fabric for your couch." "You could have done a better job." "You don't visit or ever do nice things for me." "You really disappoint me."

Furthermore, difficult parents see things only their own way. They can be demanding, curt, disagreeable, bossy people who need a lot of attention. Adult kids used words like *bitchy, controlling, complaining, explosive, unreasonable*, and *overly critical* to describe these kinds of parents. Furthermore, they noted that their difficult parents had insatiable needs, spewed relentless negative feedback, and possessed personality quirks that were hard to navigate.

One has to assume these parents might not go so far as to label even the most deserving son or daughter a poster kid, because not all of their demands or expectations are met. But by our standards, the offspring in the following cases more than qualify. Not only do they possess many of the values and qualities mentioned earlier in the chapter to describe our poster kids, but also they have to forgive more and try harder to maintain a relatively good ongoing relationship with their difficult parent.

Case #1

"My mom can make me feel like crap, and there are times when I simply have to say 'enough already.' But I don't really think she can change. She isn't going to, and I have accepted that. She used to make comments about my husband that put a lot of pressure on my marriage and made me physically sick. I went to a therapist, who told me that I needed to act like a grown-up and make my own choices. It's just that she is so strong and was always in my head. If you do something she doesn't like, she can be way nasty, short, and curt. I know she tries to make everything sound like it is your fault. I feel badly saying these things about her.

"I have dealt with the stress by avoiding issues that could get her bent out of shape and that might alienate me. I don't share a lot with her and try to do things to please her. I know it's never going to be enough, but it's less complicated and easier this way. She can make you feel guilty; it sucks! I don't think she really understands what she is doing.

"The bottom line is that she's my mother, and I am supposed to respect her. I have to listen to her, whether I love her or like her. I never want to make her feel crappy. I wouldn't be here without her. She nurtured me in her own way. I talk to her on the phone all the time and am excited when she comes to Denver to visit, except that she requires a lot of attention. We can have fun together. Sometimes I am even sad when she is leaving and don't know why. I want us to be happy and would like things to be different. I think they are a little better. I know she will always be there for me and wants me to be happy."

Case #2

"I am willing to accept my mother's behavior because I want her in my life and my kids' lives. I genuinely love her and understand why she wants to be close. There are few people in life who have that unconditional love and support for you.

"My mother has a strong and demanding personality, freaks out a lot, requires a lot of attention, makes very quick judgments about people, and reacts unpredictably to situations that can create problems.

"She has kind of weird expectations too. I am consciously aware of her expectations and make an effort to fill some of them until they become too intrusive. Like I can't talk on the phone four times a day. I am willing to give her more of what she wants because I want our relationship to be positive.

"I can understand that she is lonely since she divorced her second husband, but I am not willing to give her five nights a week. I am willing to have her over two days a week. There isn't much I can do besides treat her with compassion and kindness. I try to keep it in perspective and not make a lot out of it. Now and then, I will be honest with her and tell her she is expecting too much. That can result in her becoming very defensive. I just shove aside her reaction and move on."

A Poster Mom with Poster Kids

You are going to have a rare opportunity to meet a mom and an adult daughter in the most idyllic relationship. What these women had to say is straightforward, nonnegotiable, and valuable. The strong bond, the pleasure they take in each other's lives, and the mutual support is apparent as soon as you meet them. They may seem like an anomaly in the busy, self-centered world we inhabit, but their stories should serve as a lesson to all of us.

The Poster Daughter

"My mother is courageous, strong, and dignified. She has the biggest heart, trusts her own judgment, and has no fear of being who she is. My mom understands the world and has always been ahead of her time. I would like her a lot, even if she weren't my mom. She has given me so much with her example and wisdom.

"She was able to protect my emotional and physical well-being growing up. At the same time, she allowed me to struggle in order to learn to become accountable to myself. She wanted me to be strong, think carefully, and have my own personality. She gave us a feeling of love, acceptance, and belonging to this day. I have a strong sense of what I am supposed to do because of her.

"There is a history of hard work and meeting your responsibilities in my family. We didn't know we were poor or that our mother made sacrifices for us. When the basics are intact, you don't need a lot of money. I was taught to sacrifice and live with a sense of giving and caring.

"Our family history is one of doing whatever was necessary for the children. My grandmother told my grandfather when my mom and her sister were young that they needed a better environment to grow up in. At work one day, my grandfather, a coal miner, deliberately cut off two fingers. He had to have an excuse to leave the mines, and when my own father couldn't contribute to the family, my mom said he would have to leave. She was working so hard as a medical technician to support us. My grandmother came to live with us so that mom could work and not worry so much about us.

"We have always lived inter-generationally. Not just because of money and pulling our resources but because it is a better way of life. You can help one another and learn to depend on each other spiritually. I was a widow with three young daughters when I invited mom to move in with me.

"I need my mother to be happy, comfortable, and respected. If she needs a new car because the defroster won't work, I will get her a new car. I still feel I don't want to worry or disappoint her. My mother can do what she wants, because she is the mom and the grandmother."

The Poster Mom

"The foundation of a family must be grounded in respect. This was embedded in us at an early age. You have to teach people how to respect you. I was open-minded as a mother but had strict rules. I was not my children's friend; I was their mother. And if they broke the rules, there were consequences. When Stephanie grumbled about taking my mom to the store one day, I told her, 'You must be tired of sleeping here. Better figure out how to get her there, or don't bother coming home.' And if my children didn't speak respectfully to me, I would tell them, 'Until you figure out how to talk to me, we don't need to talk.'

"Everybody in our household deserves respect, especially those who have provided for you. We show each other kindness. There is no pretense. We say 'good morning,' 'good night,' 'excuse me,' and 'thank you.' If I am going into the kitchen to get something, I ask if someone would like something. I don't have to keep asking anyone to take out the trash, do the dishes, or rinse out the bathroom sink. We all pitch in. That and respect is understood!

"My oldest granddaughter brought her laundry home weekly from college. I was happy to do it for her. But the first time she forgot to say 'thank you,' she came back the next week and found her dirty clothes exactly where she left them. She apologized, thanked me, and never forgot the courtesy she was to afford her grandmother again."

What Our Adult Kids Can Teach Us

There are additional simple truths you need to take with you into the following chapters. As you read further and broaden your understanding, you will gain greater insight into which of these statements apply to your situation. This is a good page to mark and refer back to as you proceed through the book.

The additional simple truths are as follows:

- **Adult children don't necessarily realize they are sidelining, nor are they cognizant of your emotional needs and where you are coming from**

- Some adult children are predetermined to sideline
- Your adult children may love, honor, and respect you in wonderful ways that don't necessarily match your expectations
- Adult children have the right to be viewed as independent individuals with separate lives
- Grown children may need a refresher course in how caring families treat each other
- Parents are held to the same standards as poster kids

Your Turn to Judge

This book won't do you much good unless you stop and reflect. These are the questions you need to ask yourself at this juncture. The answers will help determine how you should handle sidelining in the future.

Critical questions

1. Do you have a poster child?
   Yes _____ No_____

2. If not, what characteristics are missing?

   _____

   _____

   _____

3. Does your child have the potential to be an adult poster child?
   Yes _____ No _____

4. If yes, what is preventing him/her from achieving this coveted status?

_____

_____

_____

5. Are you a poster parent?
   Yes_____ No_____

6. If you aren't a poster parent, what characteristics are you missing?

_____

_____

_____

7. If you aren't a poster parent at the present time, do you want to become one?
   Yes_____ No_____

What's Next?

Chapter 4 should have provided you with inspiration and possibilities. From here on, you will be offered valuable concepts, realistic goals, and professional guidance that will enable you to interact on a sound playing field with your adult children. Your task is to learn how to use this information in an open and honest way. Some of the concepts you will be reading about are parental maturity and how loving family members treat each other. Both are greatly influenced by open-mindedness.

CHAPTER 5

New and Important Concepts to Master

In order to absorb the importance and essence of the truths presented to you in this chapter, your mind needs to be open and receptive. You must give careful consideration to the concepts discussed in the next few pages. Acceptance of the ideas that follow is critical!

Holding on to ill-conceived opinions regarding parenthood, expectations, respect, and other notions that affect the relationship between you and your adult children can be hazardous for everyone. Employing these improved concepts in your daily interactions can potentially absolve you of wrongdoing, lessen your children's opportunity to sideline, and shed light on underlying family issues.

There Is No Substitute for Being Open-Minded

Open-mindedness is a state of being that some individuals come by naturally, while others have to work to achieve it. Whichever category you fall into at the moment doesn't matter as long as you sharpen or acquire the skills associated with open-mindedness. **Dealing with your adult children requires being open-minded and paves the way to better relationships.** This isn't always easy. But it is worth working on and getting right.

A Refresher Course in Being Open-Minded

Specific characteristics of being open-minded include the following:

- Acceptance of new ideas
- Facility to look at and listen to other points of view
- Tolerance for individual differences
- Capacity to agree with different approaches to the same problem
- Disposition to compromise and change one's mind
- Appreciation of different opinions
- Tendency not to be critical of others
- Capacity to acknowledge when wrong
- Willingness to give up "being right"
- Flexibility
- Aptitude to try new things

Are You Open-Minded?

Give yourself ten big points if you can honestly say you possess *all* of the characteristics above. However, before you can determine if you are really open-minded, consider whether or not the following statements apply to you.

Statement	Yes	No
1) I will not alter my opinions on matters that are very important to me.		
2) It takes a lot for me to change my mind.		
3) I prefer not to hear many new ideas.		
4) It is difficult for me to be neutral.		
5) I take it as a personal attack if people argue a point with me.		
6) It is hard for me to laugh at myself.		
7) I form firm opinions of others.		
8) I have high expectations of others.		

9) I frequently feel people who don't agree with my most
basic values are on the wrong track.

10) I rarely seek out or enjoy people with whom I am not
like-minded.

One or more check marks in the "Yes" column indicate the likelihood
that you might be a bit too narrow-minded, rigid, and self-centered. It seems
obvious that individuals who are closed-minded miss the meaning of much
of what others around them are saying or feeling. They are either unable or
unwilling to be receptive to everyday exchanges, making it difficult to forge
better workable relationships.

Becoming open-minded requires discipline and motivation. Employ both
of these, and practice being open-minded. Try to think more consciously in
line with the attributes of open-mindedness, and catch yourself when you
falter.

Enjoy the process, and notice how you feel better as you open your mind!

Warning Message for the Closed-Minded
**Heed this warning carefully: closed- and narrow-minded individuals are
strongly unreceptive to other opinions, fresh ideas, or arguments and are
unwilling to try new things. They dismiss anything that is contrary to
their own beliefs as invalid, inaccurate, or "just not me" and tend to be
critical and judgmental of others who are not like-minded.**

This type of rigid thinking, when applied to close family members,
becomes particularly hazardous to relationships. Consequently, the rigid
thinker has to work even more diligently to rid themselves of these attitudes.

Parental Maturity
It is difficult to demonstrate parental maturity unless you have gotten the
hang of being open-minded. This type of maturity is hallmarked by:

1) Acceptance of adult children and their spouses for who they are, even if they are not the people you expected or wanted them to be
2) Acknowledgment that they are grown-ups in the fullest sense of the word
3) Recognition that you do not have the right as parents to be the authority in control of their lives

Whether or not society encourages parents to reach this state of separation is debatable. After all, there isn't a word in the English language that specifically denotes "grown-up offspring." Instead, parents refer to their progeny as kids or children without any distinction regarding age as newborns, toddlers, adolescents, adults, or seniors all of their lives!

How Loving Family Members Treat Each Other
Loving family members are authentically kind, caring, and respectful with a desire to be close and spend time together, Pat says.

Now that sounds like an easy prescription to follow, and one many parents and offspring alike believe is fulfilling. The catch is that the words *loving*, *kind*, and *caring* may have different interpretations among family members. When these interpretations are out of sync, there is the risk of parents feeling sidelined.

Important Definitions for Loving Family Members
It is always a good idea to make sure that you and your adult children are speaking the same language when it comes to discussing the state of your family.

Love and Like
Although romantic love is ethereal and hard to describe, love in the more practical sense has common characteristics we can easily pinpoint. According to dictionary definitions and psychologists, *love* implies a great attachment to, affection toward, and commitment to another person. The intensity of that love

is underscored by a sympathetic consciousness of and compassion for another person's happiness or distress and the desire to make life better for that individual.

Liking implies a fondness for someone whose company provides enjoyment. What liking does not have that love does is the same level of commitment. **Both loving and liking, however, form the basis of family relationships that are authentically close, caring, and kind.**

When duty or a sense of responsibility, rather than genuine loving and liking, foster acts of caring and kindness, they may be less authentic but can still be satisfying. We interviewed adult children who didn't particularly like a parent but who expressed a sense of parental love and were, therefore, committed to being caring sons or daughters.

Caring

A genuinely caring individual is sensitive and empathetic enough to be aware of and respectful of someone's needs and feelings. This individual demonstrates sincere concern and compassion by offering support.

People who are trapped in their own bodies and lives, Pat emphasizes, generally do not possess the level of empathy necessary to initiate authentic acts of caring. They may feel obliged to show support in some instances but do not naturally perform caring acts.

Although caring can be demonstrated by someone who doesn't necessarily love or like the individual recipient, most parents can feel the difference when such acts are heartfelt. And while most moms and dads would hope for the heartfelt acts, they graciously accept acts inspired by obligation.

Kindness

To show kindness encompasses being nice, thoughtful, considerate, helpful, and sympathetic. Inherently kind individuals are warm hearted and empathetic. They are motivated to do nice things for others out of the genuine desire to make them happy rather than out of a sense of duty or promoting an image of themselves. However, even the so-called "inherently kind" individual may not be motivated to extend acts of kindness to someone he or she does not like.

There are other important parameters to kindness that Pat likes to pull into this discussion. For instance, everyone needs to be kind to him- or herself. Because kindness is often seen in terms of giving, the inherently kind person may have to set limits in order not to become a victim of someone else's desires.

Surrendering your own life, putting aside what is important to you, becoming a doormat, or feeling like a martyr means you are giving too much and not being kind to yourself.

Closeness

To be close to another individual means feeling friendship, inseparability, openness, and affection for him or her, in addition to having a deep understanding of and loyalty to that person. Individuals who are close to one another feel comfortable enough to bond through self-disclosure. There is no faking true closeness. It requires honesty, self-exposure, and acceptance—tall orders for family members.

Respect

Respect is primarily given by (a) showing esteem for someone whom you admire for their abilities or achievements, (b) exhibiting deference for an individual who is in a privileged position or on a higher level, or (c) valuing a person for their uniqueness. All of these expressions of respect are equally valuable.

Some parents expect their children to treat them with deference as if they are on a higher plain. Respect in our book does not mean having to do something exactly the way a parent wants or thinks an adult child should. **Respecting one's parent because they are good, selfless, caring people who provided for the family unit denotes greater personal appreciation of the individual and may result in kids more easily letting go of negativity or judgments.** That's the kind of respect that discourages sidelining and that loving family members exhibit toward one another.

Respect in any format is welcomed into the adult child–parent relationship and is likely to contribute to behavior that demonstrates feelings of appreciation, empathy, and concern for each other's well being.

Getting Real about Loving Families

We are not taking back what we said about "loving families." However, **there is no super happy family with the perfect connections all the time.** There just isn't. That's part of life.

To get through the ups and downs, loving family members must:

1) Respect and accept each other's limitations and issues
2) Relinquish excessive expectations
3) Love each other, even when someone isn't lovable
4) Deal with the negativity and not take it too seriously
5) Try to understand where the other person is coming from
6) Tolerate one another
7) Learn to be together positively
8) Let go of anger or grievances
9) Learn not to take their own issues out on someone else
10) Talk and work problems out when they arise
11) Come to terms with all of it

Family members who behave in this manner don't run the risk of alienating themselves or someone else.

How to Make a Legitimate Request

Here is where even loving family members can get into trouble! Being a loving family member does not require that everyone does everything that is asked of them. Sometimes we request too much of each other.

A legitimate request:

1) Asks rather than demands
2) Respects other family members' time and commitments
3) Does not put pressure on family members
4) Encourages the other person to tell if there is a conflict with a request and negotiate a solution if needed

5) Always leaves the door open for a family member to say, "I cannot do that" or "no"

For example, expecting your children and grandchildren to spend time with you or come for weekly dinners is legitimate. However, when schedules conflict or there are times our adult children cannot fulfill these expectations, we would hope that both parents and adult children would try to work this out and reach a healthy understanding in a friendly way.

To avert the trap of excessive demands or expectations, it is healthier to "wish" or to "want" to be important in your children's lives, to know them, and for them to really know you. In other words, to have a reasonably conflict-free, meaningful, fun, and open relationship with our adult children is a legitimate desire; but it is best if you express this as what you want or wish, not necessarily what you expect.

What the Unloving Family Looks Like

Family members who do not seem to have the ability to be a part of a loving circle are usually easy to spot. These individuals generally manifest some of the following behaviors:

- They often are ready to point a finger at somebody
- They prefer doing their own thing to family get-togethers
- They do not appear to value extended family
- They do not readily offer support to family members
- They are often self-centered, angry, side-taking blamers
- They tend to have unfair expectations of one another
- They seem to be close-minded and judgmental
- They may rely on guilt to make others do as they wish

Even just one of the characteristics can cause a fatal blow to the family unit.

Assessing Your Family

Social and cultural forces, plus each family member's individual characteristics, affect the family environment. It is within this milieu that we interact, form relationships, and potentially become committed, supportive family members. Keep this in mind as you determine the state of your family and whether or not there is enough mutual desire to change your family for the better.

Step #1

Consider how well your family fares when compared with the attributes of loving and unloving families listed above. Does your family qualify as loving and caring? Yes _____ No_____

Step #2

List your family's strengths and weaknesses:

Strengths

1) _____

_____

2) _____

_____

3) _____

_____

4) _____

_____

Weaknesses

1) _____

_____

2) _____

_____

3) _____

_____

4) _____

_____

Step#3
List gestures of loving behavior among family members that could be improved:

1) _____

_____

2) _____

_____

3) _____

_____

4) _____

_____

Step#4

List behavior you might personally change that could contribute to a more harmonious, loving family atmosphere:

1) _____

_____

2) _____

_____

3) _____

_____

4) _____

_____

Beliefs You May Not Want to Give Up but Should

There are three major assumptions parents often make that need to be expelled from your belief system before you go on to the next chapter. If you harbor these misconceptions, now is a good time to give them up. They will not serve you well now or in the future.

Read slowly and carefully—several times, if you must—to grasp the fine distinctions made for your benefit.

Strike Belief #1: Parents Can Mold Their Children

Moms and dads assume they have an inordinate amount of influence over their children's personalities and future. The plain fact is, Pat says, it's just not true.

But try to tell that to the mother of the groom at a bridal shower, who boasted, "My kids are wonderful. I did a great job."

On the other hand, a woman feeling neglected, unloved, and rejected by her daughter grimly repeated over and over, "I don't know what I did wrong raising her that she could be so heartless toward me."

Although the argument between nature and nurture is still relatively fluid, nature seems to be gaining ground. Suffice it to say for our present focus that although parents generally are the most significant adults in their children's lives, they have much less influence over their offspring than they realize.

Several other factors have come to light over the past twenty years, based upon a plethora of twin studies, particularly those of identical twins raised in different homes. Uncanny similarities in behavior and personality provide these researchers with evidence that genetic factors have a huge influence on development.

Pulitzer Prize–winning researcher Judith Rich Harris, PhD, author of *The Nurture Assumption: Why Children Turn Out the Way They Do*, proposed that peer groups may have more influence than parents. Pat agrees that the schools our adult children went to, groups they participated in, and the culture they were raised in have a huge effect on their lives. All of this is even truer today.

It is particularly important that parents acknowledge the limitations of their own influence. What you could give your kids was nurturance, acceptance, discipline, and structure. You simply didn't create who your children were or became. Rather, you should hope that in a healthy manner, you facilitated their growth the best way you could without over-identifying with them and wanting them to be more like you.

This is a very hard job. **We assume way too much responsibility when we think we determine our adult children's choices.**

Strike Belief #2: Adult Children Will Fulfill Their Parents' Expectations

In ten out of ten cases, your adult children will not meet all of your expectations. And it's not their fault. Don't let it be yours either.

The expectation that if you raise your children in a loving and caring way, they will treat you in a similar manner when they reach adulthood is incorrect. All you have to do is look at all the sidelined parents in today's world.

Whether an expectation is or is not legitimate, this generation of adult children often struggle with our expectations and hear them as demands or a reflection of our neediness. When parental expectations are perceived as particularly excessive or inflexible, adult offspring frequently begin to avoid their parents or become explosive and defensive.

One of the worst things parents can do to drive their children into sidelining is openly express or demonstrate disapproval when their expectations are not met. One mother admitted she absolutely expresses her disapproval. She believed it was her right. The problem is that she has a major sidelining issue with her daughter, who tries at all costs to avoid her mother and her expressions of disapproval.

Strike Belief #3: Parenting Is an Implicit Bargain

"I spent twenty years of my life giving you everything, doing everything for you, and now you treat me like crap," many parents typically expressed. What they were implying is that one should get something back for being a devoted parent.

It is natural (whether conscious or not) to feel this way, but it is not realistic, Pat emphasizes. That's why it takes some work to let these implicit expectations go.

My husband certainly thinks this way. We were watching a commercial that showed a bald eagle steadfastly sitting on a nest of eggs with just her head poking out of a mound of freezing snow. After seeing this, my husband looked over at me and sarcastically said, "Do you think they will ever say 'thank you'?"

The implicit bargaining ideology doesn't do parents any good. Let it go, and finally accept that there is no intrinsic reward in parenting! **Sorry, there is no correlation between good parenting and getting something back from your children.**

Scrap these notions:

1) "I gave my kids everything and expect something in return."
2) "Because I was a good parent, I will have children who treat me nicely."
3) "I love my kids; consequently, they will love me."

You need to view being a parent this way: the mere recognition or act of being a good parent who is generous and caring is your primary reward, Pat tells her clients.

In general, giving to others and being kind is intrinsically rewarding and leads to peace of mind and happiness. It also contributes to being guilt free when problems arise. Guilt free is a wonderful thing to strive for!

That is how we need to look at parenting for our own well-being. We acknowledge this isn't easy, particularly for our generation that was hugely attentive and focused on our kids.

What's Next?

What you learn in the next chapter can be applied to everything you experience. It is particularly relevant when trying to get out from under negative behavior directed toward you by your adult children. Accepting how your feelings and reactions develop within yourself enables you to go one step further and choose how you want to feel. It sounds more difficult than it is. But you may need to reread and consider the following chapter several times before you get it!

CHAPTER 6

A Crash Course in Understanding
Feelings and Behavior

D r. James is a "responsibility therapist." Responsibility therapy encourages individuals to take responsibility for their own feelings.

In order to be able to do that, you must have a good understanding of specific feelings. This is a prerequisite for working through conflict with your adult children.

Chapter 6 is full of new concepts related to your thoughts, feelings, and actions. You may be resistant to some of these ideas at first. Keep your mind open, and work hard to digest these new concepts. They are the solid building blocks that will prepare you to take charge of your thoughts and feelings, eventually moving you into a happier place.

Accepting Responsibility for the Origin of Your Reactions

Your reactions probably don't arise in the way you think they do. Accepting the correct evolution of your reactions and feelings will require surrendering old beliefs. We will walk you through the process step by step and succinctly present concepts you need to master.

Take time to digest six new ideas that hold a key to your happiness.

Idea # 1: Thoughts create feelings; your thoughts create your own feelings.

Idea # 2: Your adult children's behavior does not create your uncomfortable feelings. Your feelings come from your own thoughts and your own interpretation of events.

Idea # 3: In order to change your feelings, you must accept the basic premises put forth in 1 & 2.

Idea # 4: To change your feelings, you need to recognize what it is you are thinking after being sidelined. This is hard because our thoughts are both conscious and unconscious. If you are not sure what you are thinking, just guess! A guess is better than saying you just don't know. It means you are trying to get at what is on your mind.

Idea #5: We love to blame others for how we feel. It is part of our "humanness" to get off the hook. It makes us the innocent party, a victim. It makes the other person the jerk. That's much easier than assuming responsibility for our own thoughts and feelings.

Idea #6: If you want to be happy, you must stop blaming others (like your children) for how you feel and take responsibility for your own feelings.

An Emotional Chain of Events

Keep this model in mind. It is how your brain works within seconds of a sidelining infraction:

First link: you are the recipient of an external action (words or behavior directed at you from an external source).

Second link: you experience internal thoughts (thoughts that arise as a response to an external action).

Third link: you develop feelings (an emotional state formulated by your thoughts).

Fourth link: you convey a reaction (a response that is determined by your thoughts and feelings).

Let's apply this to sidelining: **to change your reaction when sidelined, you must first alter your thoughts and choose how you want to feel.**

You will need to keep reading carefully through the next few sections to get a good handle on this chain reaction.

Clarifying Examples
Being hurt is not pure emotion. It is a combination of a thought and a feeling.

Example #1: Make a Choice
Decide which of these parents you would rather be:

A. "My daughter did something hurtful that made me feel pain rather than doing something nice that could make me feel good."
B. "My son never spends a Mother's Day with me. He follows his wife to her mother's. I wish I could be with him, but I am not going to allow his decision to upset me."

We hope you chose B!

Example #2: The Perpetually Upset Mother-in-Law
Negative reactions and bad feelings when sidelined become habitual and may rob you of clear, mature, and productive thoughts—not to mention your happiness.

Just the other day, I had a mother tell me how she wished she didn't get so distressed by her son's wife. Most recently, her daughter-in-law told her to pick between coming for a short visit to attend her granddaughter's end-of-school-year program and coming to Father's Day at their home several weeks later.

This furious mother-in-law felt victimized yet again by her daughter-in-law. We assume that her thoughts went like this:

"I hate what she just said. It is nasty and unfair. She is always upsetting me. She makes me miserable. She ruins everything for me."

Fortunately, the perpetually upset mother did not respond negatively on the spot. But she was still rattled when reporting the incident to us.

"The audacity of her. Can you imagine such a thing? Why can't I come to both? My husband and I would be happy to make the trip twice. It was all I could do not to scream at her. I have before. This time, I got off the phone and steamed for days. I am still steaming. She upsets me to no end, and my son does nothing about it. I am hurt and frustrated by her all the time. She constantly pulls these things. How can I possibly make the choice between having my husband spend Father's Day without his son and telling my granddaughter I cannot make it to her program? I will feel miserable no matter what I decide and won't enjoy either visit. Why does she do this to me?"

Blaming Others instead of Taking Responsibility for How You Feel

We know people are resistant to taking responsibility for their feelings and might not readily want to accept this fact. It is easier to think you are angry or hurt because of the way someone treated you. In other words, "It's their fault I am feeling so crummy."

It isn't easy to stop blaming your kids for how you feel. Pat gets that initial reaction all the time from clients: "You mean I shouldn't be furious when my kids treat me like dirt? Are you kidding? They're the ones who are doing something wrong! Not me! You would be pissed off too. If our kids acted nicely, we would be fine."

Sure, you can believe this, but it won't make you happy!

We all want validation that it was our kid who made us feel so crappy. People want to believe that *external* events cause their feelings. The truth is, external events only *trigger* thoughts that are already there.

Giving up resistance to blaming others for how you feel is difficult. It takes time, effort, understanding, and practice. We will help you reach this critical plateau, because taking responsibility saves you a lot of grief and will make you happier! Only you can choose to change how you think and feel. It is well worth the effort to master this concept. You cannot change how others act or behave, but you can control your own thoughts, feelings, actions, and behaviors.

For the moment, however, let's look at how the perpetually upset-mother-in-law could have reacted when her daughter-in-law gave her that either-or invite.

"I do not like what my daughter-in-law just said. I think it is nasty and unfair. I am going to stay calm and instead ask her, 'Is there a reason you are inviting us for one weekend or the other? We would be happy to come in for both.'"

If the situation did not work out to her liking, rather than being upset, this mother-in-law needed to tell herself this: "I don't have to allow my daughter-in-law's behavior to cause me to feel angry and unhappy. I am responsible for my own feelings. I determine how I want to feel. I choose to be happy and don't want to waste my time or energy on feeling miserable. This is not how I would like things to be, but it is what it is. I think it would be nice to go in for the school program and have an early Father's Day celebration. I will suggest that. No matter what happens, I am going to enjoy the time with my granddaughter and my son! On Father's Day, I will plan to do something special for my husband. I want to be happy!"

Taking Responsibility Feels Good and Has Positive Side Effects

My daughters may be able to pinpoint when I began to take responsibility for my own feelings. My behavior, attitude, and comfort level changed drastically. Self-regulating my behavior, being less reactive, and taking responsibility for my feelings have turned me into a nicer and more content mother of adult children.

"I don't think you are letting it hurt you so much if we make choices that used to upset you," acknowledged my younger daughter. "And you seem a lot happier. You have done a lot of work, and I really appreciate it. It has made a big impact on our relationship. I know it isn't an easy thing to monitor how you to talk to me, but it has made it easier for me to share more things in my life with you. I know that you aren't coming from a place of judgment. This is a huge change for me as well."

It's true. Once I saw the light and decided to be more open-minded and take responsibility for my own feelings, there was a calm about me that had not been there before. Sure, I can get off the phone and bitch for a few moments or vent to my husband or friend—but nothing more. I don't want to be one of the miserable people; I don't want to be unhappy, and I am not going to let anyone spoil my day!

The last time one of my daughters declined to accept an invitation to a celebratory family dinner I strongly thought she should attend, I voiced my opinion as nicely as I could and told her we would like her to go with us, but I didn't belabor the point. Before I got the hang of this responsibility thing, I would have been furious for weeks, taken her decision personally, probably gotten into an argument, and stewed about it until after the event.

Instead, I chose not to get upset and told myself, "I don't like her decision. In my opinion, it is wrong, and I don't understand it. But it's her decision. I am not responsible for what my adult children do or don't do. I am going to enjoy myself." And I did.

The Anatomy of Anger

Pat is insistent that 100 percent of the time, when individuals express anger, there is another issue involved on a deeper level.

An angry outburst is an action of your reactive self and may appear to make you look tough and powerful. But in reality, **at the deepest level, anger is a superficial, ill considered, and generally an impulsive defense to cover up or manage pain.** The point is that you can choose to change your thoughts and, therefore, alter how you feel. You don't have to be angry unless you want to!

Here is how anger develops:

External Action → Internal Defensive Thoughts → Feeling of Anger

An Example of How Anger Works

Kathleen's daughter had not called or responded to her mother's messages for days. When Kathleen, a widow, finally did get through to her daughter, she said, "If you don't ever call, how will you know I am alive?"

Kathleen's daughter coolly and sarcastically remarked, "I'll know when you've died."

Within seconds, Kathleen was grievously wounded and angry. She shouted, "Why the f - - k are you so mean and nasty to me?" Then, she slammed down the phone. In its simplest form, here is how Kathleen's response took shape:

A Nasty Remark → Internal Thoughts of Being Unloved, Unworthy, and Rejected → Feelings of Anger

Looking beneath one's anger, there is frequently a degree of fear, sadness, or loss that needs to be recognized before you can take responsibility for your feelings and produce a more positive reaction. In Kathleen's instance, she was fearful that her daughter didn't love or like her. Additionally, Kathleen had just learned that a friend her age died alone at home and was not found until three days later by her adult children.

Anger Prohibits Positive Responses

When you allow anger to become the go-to response, you are robbing yourself of clear thinking and the ability to control your emotions. Getting stuck in a reaction like anger denies the opportunity to get in touch with what you are really feeling.

In Kathleen's case, recognizing that in all probability, her feeling of anger was reactive and based upon specific fears, she could have had the wherewithal to consider what problem she had triggered in her daughter and how she might better deal with it. For instance, realizing that her daughter's response was totally inappropriate, she might have asked why her remark upset her so much and explain why she herself was particularly sensitive at this point in time for no one checking on her.

Applying this rational thinking and foregoing anger in all types of situations opens the possibility for understanding, forgiving, and talking.

Being Mean Is a Cover-Up

Many parents have expressed that their children treat them in a mean, nasty, or vindictive way. These parents have taken this personally by withdrawing or carrying grudges and sometimes escalating the negativity. Maybe what they need to know is that individuals aren't mean unless they are struggling internally.

Meanness comes from a person's own pain.

When adult children meanly lash out at you, it suggests one of several things. They are probably:

1) Unhappy about something
2) Feeling bad about themselves
3) Stressed out

When you are able to take responsibility for your feelings and not get upset with adult children who are angry or mean, you will be better positioned to be loving and caring and help get to the bottom of their pain.

For example, Olivia called her daughter to make plans to get together with the grandchildren. Her request set off a vitriolic explosion in her daughter: "Do you have nothing to do all day but call me, Mother? The kids aren't available this week!

Do you think the world revolves around your requests?"

Olivia wisely squelched her initial, fleeting thought that her daughter was a huge, disrespectful brat who was never going to be nice to her. Knowing this bolt of meanness represented a problem her daughter must be having, Olivia gave the issue back to her daughter where it belonged.

"Sounds like you're having a pretty bad day. Anything I can do to help? If not, we can talk about this later. Bye."

Understandably, Olivia's response took a lot of self-control, awareness, empathy, and practice. But it saved her from dissolving into tears and misery, prevented her from ruining her own day, and enabled her to extend a helping hand.

Happiness Is Not a Constant State of Being

No one is happy all of the time. If you expect to be happy all the time, you are expecting to be superhuman.

The Peaks and Valleys of Happiness

Some people think that happiness is a feeling of euphoria that is achieved when you have most of what you want. **Pat prefers to equate happiness with a deep sense of contentment, peace of mind, and knowing that you are pretty much okay.**

There are two distinct types of people who inhabit our world: the happy people and the miserable people. The miserable people complain, blame, act grouchy, do not take responsibility for their own happiness, and rarely exhibit the characteristics of happy people. The happy people are basically individuals who smile, find joy in living, do not dwell on the negatives, and take responsibility for feelings that might impinge upon or damper their overall happiness. They certainly experience feeling anxiety and guilt and even shed their share of tears, but ultimately, their natural state is to feel okay and be content. They don't clog up their lives with all the junk that miserable people do.

Take heart if you are one of the miserable people. You don't have to stay that way. You can learn to become one of the happy people and even manage to eliminate the negative effects of being sidelined.

Sadness Is a Part of Life

Sadness is one of those normal, natural emotions that everyone struggles with, Pat says. You don't necessarily feel it consciously every day, but it is always there at some unconscious level.

Acute sadness can disrupt feelings of happiness, but it doesn't have to turn you into a sad person. Most bouts of sadness are temporary and don't hurl you into a serious state of depression. Although some people tend to describe themselves as mildly depressed when they feel sad, real depression is an ongoing state that affects your entire life.

Many parents interviewed expressed a sense of sadness when their relationship or interactions with their adult children didn't go as they planned or imagined. A particularly soft spoken, sensitive, and gentle father expressed profound sadness over his relationship with his adult son. He envisioned a warm, welcoming atmosphere in his married son's home, a close family relationship with his daughter-in-law, intimate verbal exchanges, and overt signs of affection—none of which reflected his present reality. If he and his wife were denied a meaningful role in their forthcoming grandchild's life, he vowed to move out of town rather than face such daily disappointment.

"If I am going to be sad, I might as well be sad somewhere else close to other family members," this dad expressed.

His sadness acknowledged the potential loss of the relationship he had looked forward to with his adult son and caused a feeling of grief similar to what one experiences when losing a friend or family member. A heaviness of heart, sense of sorrow, and even twinges of helplessness, emptiness, and pain all describe a normal grieving process.

Fortunately, once this wise, introspective man accepted the presence of his sadness (and, with the help of his wife, didn't get stuck in it), he recognized that feeling sad did not have to preclude real joy. Within time, he completed the process of grieving, adjusted to his loss, and regained his happy, healthy self.

Overcoming grief is an integral part of surviving and thriving sidelining, particularly when you come to the conclusion that your relationship with your adult child is never going to be what you hoped for.

Controlling or Manipulative Behavior

Individuals who are controlling may be self-centered and selfish, lack sufficient empathy and self-esteem, or simply be anxious and fearful. **Anxiety and fear drive much of what appears to be controlling or manipulative behavior.**

It is worthwhile for us to grasp these dynamics in light of the fact that many parents expressed going head to head with adult children who either exhibited this behavior or accused their parents of being controlling or manipulative.

Being manipulative is trying to get what you want in a deceptive way. Whether this is a conscious or unconscious act, the motivation is the same, and the individuals who use this type of behavior do not believe they can get the results they want by being honest or straightforward.

For instance, if their job requires them to do something or be someplace they are uncomfortable with, rather than expose their feelings of inadequacy, they will fabricate a lie that excuses their participation. The fear of being found out or chastised is greater than the discomfort of lying.

A number of parents believed their offspring had been and still were manipulated by dominant spouses in a way that encouraged sidelining and resulted in family breakups. A young woman whose brother had become estranged from his entire family blamed her sister-in-law for feeding her sibling lies about his family's behavior toward her until she managed to completely extract him from his family.

"I really think his wife was afraid he might prefer us to her. By getting rid of us, she didn't have to worry about that," the sister told us.

We have interviewed families in which it became clear that adult children severely restricted access to their kids for fear that spoiling by the grandparents might cause their little ones to like them better.

Controlling or manipulative behavior explains some of the sidelining parents are experiencing.

A footnote: Control should not be misconstrued only as a behavior with negative connotations. It is much more complex. **The positive side of control (the one to be championed) is taking power over your own life. That's the kind of control we want you to gain from this book.**

The Multiple Interpretations of Judgmental Behavior

Making judgments is a tricky business and something our adult kids say we do way too frequently. To them, judgments have a negative connotation, encompass opinions we want to impose upon them, and imply they are doing something wrong. Judgments that fit their description get in the way of loving and caring.

Not All Judgments Are Negative

All of us are entitled to our own opinions. We shouldn't be afraid to express ourselves sometimes, although nearly all parents we interviewed were highly selective about what they did or did not say to their adult kids.

They anticipated that their adult offspring would interpret their opinion as a criticism or judgment directed toward them. In many instances, these parents were right. Adult kids still want parental approval. When they feel they aren't getting it, they worry that they are wrong.

There were other parents who feared that if their opinions were construed as a criticism, their children would punish them by withholding the grandchildren or refusing to talk to them.

Adult children should be grown up enough to realize the following:

- Not all parental opinions or judgments are loaded with hidden meanings
- No one can get through a day without some making some judgments
- Judgments may be complimentary or neutral in nature
- Everyone makes judgments, even when they are blaming you for being judgmental

The Two-Sided Coin of Being Judgmental

One day I received an email from my younger daughter, who accused me of being judgmental and said that she would have to steer clear of discussing specific topics with me because my comments were overloaded with judgments. Like many parents, I was tired of being found guilty of something I felt wasn't quite fair. It was time to stand my ground.

I sent back an email saying, "I am tired of being called judgmental. You are the one being judgmental. What makes you so right that you can make that judgment call? When you can accept that I am a person with opinions, we can talk."

Because she is an open-minded and loving daughter, she wrote back, "You are right. I apologize."

I am not so sure either of us would have handled this situation quite as well had I not already done my work and accepted responsibility for my own feelings.

Mom's Dilemma

While we won't get into the whole mother-daughter issue, there are two factors that are particularly pertinent to our topic. Parents with married sons may envy mothers with daughters, but the reality is that the complexities of the mother-daughter bond can make the relationship just as toxic and difficult as that with a daughter-in-law.

There are two primary reasons for this.

Reason #1

Daughters don't seem to separate completely from their mothers. As a result, daughters:

1) Endow their mothers with a lot of power
2) Expect their moms to always say and do the right thing
3) Assume their moms will promote their happiness, even at the expense of her own
4) Imagine that their moms will be able to accept everything they say or do, even when it is hurtful

5) Place more blame on or express more anger toward their mothers than anyone else

The crux of the matter is that if mothers weren't endowed with so much power, it is conceivable there wouldn't be as many problems between them and their daughters.

Reason #2
Moms are the alter egos of their female offspring. This results in the following:

1) The more a daughter likes herself, the more she should like her mother
2) If a daughter doesn't like herself all that much, she doesn't like her mom either and projects all of her negativity onto her mother
3) Daughters have the unconscious habit of always comparing themselves to their mothers, either fearing they are coming up short or that they might be like them

All of the ramifications of being alter egos place mom in a tenuous position.

Over-Identifying with Our Adult Children

Of course we love our kids, want them to be an integral part of our lives, and enjoy the pleasure of their attention and company as adults. When they were young, they provided us with happiness, consumed our resources, and were in many cases the center of our universe. Why wouldn't we be sad after they moved away or shut us out of their lives as adults? Our love for them is overwhelming.

Perhaps, however, our feelings arise much more out of over-identifying with our adult children and caring too much about our relationships, giving them excessive influence over our happiness quotient.

We do this way too much!

Our questionnaires certainly corroborated her opinion that we are too connected with our kids in a way that sometimes prevents us from being happy. Parents who felt excessively unhappy as a result of their adult children's sidelining behavior were overly affected by this behavior and even felt it was their kids' job to make them happy.

Equally impacted were parents whose adult children's difficulties or successes made them either markedly unhappy or happy. We can't tell you how many times parents quoted the old adage "I am as happy as my least happy child."

Remarkably, a psychiatrist we spoke to should have recognized the extent to which she was overly identifying with her son. When asked how he was doing, she replied, "You can always tell just by looking at me."

The bottom line is, you need a life beyond your kids!

What's Next?

You are ready to move onto Part III, where you will be introduced to Pat's prescription for happiness. You will look at ways to get in touch with your own feelings, learn how to talk things over with your adult children, find tools to help solve problems, and take charge of your life and your future.

Part III: Taking Charge

Warning:

Don't even think about reading Part III first! You need every morsel of information that has been carefully presented for you in previous chapters! This information provides the foundation upon which you will take charge, oversee your relationship with your adult children, and find the peace, contentment, and happiness you deserve.

Part III will lead you through a process of introspection and teach you how to assume control over your responses to sidelining, when and how to engage your adult children in meaningful conversations, and finally, how to move on in a manner that is best for you.

Liberating yourself from pain and disappointment is a process that requires patience and understanding. Happiness won't be found attempting to validate your misery by trying to prove that your children are wrong and then laying blame for your misery at their doorstep—even if you have been grievously mistreated, which many parents have been.

Understandably, this isn't a simple task!

Initially, I tried to coax Pat into acknowledging that parents are completely innocent and rightfully aggrieved. She would not give an inch, except to admit that feeling hurt, angry, disappointed, or neglected when sidelined by adult children is natural but not healthy or productive. She is nonetheless sympathetic to your pain and disappointment. She's had her share of both, and she refuses to point a finger in a one-way direction. After all, doing so would sabotage all attempts to create a realistic relationship with your adult children or prevent you from acknowledging what you can or cannot change.

Your primary goal remains determining what is best for you and finding the strength of conviction to meet your own needs.

CHAPTER 7

Take a Hard Look in the Mirror

What you need to keep in mind as you read and react to this self-examination is that the objective is not to place blame in your lap for the sidelining antics being inflicted upon you. **We would prefer to drop the word blame altogether! There is no room for blaming in this book.**

The purpose is to get to the root of how and why these sidelining machinations affect you. Without this process of introspection, you will be missing a strong element that is essential to freeing yourself from pain and adequately separating from your adult offspring.

Much of what is offered here is also helpful to use when looking at your "sideliner" and trying to determine what is his or her problem. Adult kids would also benefit by taking a long, hard look in the mirror. But that's their job, not yours!

Sharpen your pencil, and get ready to attack the abundant worksheets throughout this chapter.

Pat's Prescription

You have learned enough to realize that individual reactions to external behavior are more than skin deep; they go below the surface, and so must you. Only in this way can you begin to fill Pat's prescription to **take responsibility for your own emotions.**

This is a daunting task. There is evidence that great thinkers as far back as Greek philosopher Epictetus, two thousand years ago, advised against blaming others when anxious or troubled. He believed that these feelings originate within us.

The same applies to sidelined parents.

Undoubtedly, this notion may not be easily accepted.

One sidelined dad said, "What do you mean my feelings come from me? My kids piss me off. Why wouldn't I be mad?"

The problem is that he was still angry and hurt from sidelining that occurred years ago.

So give this theory a chance before you dismiss it. Would you rather be a pissed-off, miserable parent or a happier, healthier human being not eaten up with self-imposed grief?

Fortunately, through continuous coaching and absorbing the ideas in our book, this once-angry man is beginning to see the light. "I get it—well, most of it, not all of it.

"Determining how I want to feel and finding out why I have carried such anger lifts the burden of the past and gives me a way out. It's refreshing. I hate to admit it, but I think I feel better."

Poor Connections

There were many adult parents who, like this dad, said, "My children hurt me," or "My child makes me unhappy." When Pat didn't readily side with them and blame their children for their misery, some moms and dads were confused. But the fact is that **offering sympathy is not the cure for what ails sidelined parents—taking responsibility for your feelings is.**

This is a big step for all of us.

We have been taught from an early age that others cause us to feel hurt, sad, or angry, thereby making the connection between someone else's action and our feelings. In other words, we learned that something external, something outside of ourselves, causes an emotional response that we have no control over.

For instance, when one child rebuffs another's attempt to engage him or her on the playground, we might say to the pouting child, "Oh, did he hurt your feelings?"

The same sort of disconnect is applied when it comes to your children. You may say your child hurt you, but that isn't exactly correct. You may not like what your child has said or done to you, but it is you who is allowing yourself to feel hurt.

Fortunately, we can create new connections between external behavior and our inner thoughts, and we can create healthier feelings of our own choosing.

Making New Connections

A greater understanding of human emotion has uncovered the potential for individuals to determine their own responses and feelings in the quest to create happier lives.

Richard Davidson, PhD, professor of psychology at the University of Wisconsin and author of *The Emotional Life of Your Brain*, has studied this phenomenon for forty years. Cognitive therapy and mindful meditation are, according to Davidson, two of the means by which an individual can achieve better control over these responses and feelings.

Scientific studies confirm that our brains have more plasticity than was previously thought and therefore enable us to change. Rerouting pathways of neurons and creating different brain associations facilitates our ability to direct new behaviors and thinking that can optimize happiness.

In other words, by being consistently thoughtful and diligent, you too can construct new connections in your brain to replace those that previously diminished your happiness by pairing sidelining with misery and angst.

To our point, take a look at this example. If you used to be one of those wilting parents who automatically felt angry, betrayed, saddened, and disrespected when their adult kid engaged in unwelcoming behavior, you can break and make a new connection. Practice will reinforce the desired results.

Begin by:

1) Accepting that your emotional responses come from within yourself
2) Denying the old pathway that connects sidelining to self-pity, sadness, and victimization
3) Creating a new pathway that prompts you to choose how you wish to feel

Try it out to create better connections for yourself. It's simply a matter of your choosing. We will guide you through the process.

Test Your Emotional Responsibility Level

The purpose of this quiz is to evaluate how much further you have to go to take control of your feelings and reactions.

Check the column that most accurately reflects whether a statement applies to you.

Statement   **Yes   No**

1. I use the word *hurt* to describe how I feel.
2. I become upset if people fail to treat me in a kind and caring way.
3. I think my happiness depends on people being nice to me.
4. I find that other people can ruin my day.
5. I carry my grievances and grudges into the future.
6. I don't readily forgive and forget.
7. I don't feel valued if someone is rude to me.
8. I tend to take things personally.
9. I am generally defensive.
10. I blame others for making me miserable.

Your job is to work on changing every yes to a no. These are not healthy responses because:

- They encourage self-pity instead of responsibility for your own feelings

- They ascribe way too much power to others to affect your well-being
- They rob you of the opportunity to take charge and be happy

Improving Your Responsibility Level

Before delving into your emotional self and uncovering factors that might be blocking you from assuming ownership of your feelings, you have two lists of behaviors that need to be incorporated into your everyday life. They are "Golden Rules" and "Healthy Choices." Each rule you abide by and every healthy choice you make will promote better pathways that help you take control and responsibility for your feelings.

The Golden Rules

These rules are your guiding light and will help you make better choices when tackling issues pertaining to your emotional self. Until you get the hang of using these "Golden Rules," keep copies of them in your wallet, on your desk, or any other handy place where they are readily available. You will need a constant reminder to adhere to these rules until they become your modus operandi and guide your choices and behavior.

The "Golden Rules"

1. I can change the way I feel.
2. I want to be happy.
3. I can make myself feel better by not being reactive and by dealing with my deeper concerns.
4. I will not allow other people to have power over my feelings.
5. I will let go of whatever part of a relationship makes me unhappy.
6. I will accept what I have no control over.

Follow the "Golden Rules" without exception!

Making Healthy Choices

Here are some of the kinds of choices you can make no matter what behavior you are confronted with. Circle the choices you would want to make for yourself.

You can decide if you want to:

1) Linger in pain and disappointment or let it go
2) Be sad or happy
3) Blame others for your misery or take responsibility for your own feelings
4) Replace anger with peace of mind
5) Be a self-sacrificing martyr or self-preservationist
6) Be a doormat or a strong, empowered individual and parent
7) Rely on others to meet your needs or make yourself happy
8) Accept what is, rather than insist on how life ought to be
9) Get stuck trying to change the external or manage your internal self
10) Allow yourself to be victim or victor

The choices that are best for you should be obvious. Those are the choices you want to make today and every day hereafter. It will be beneficial for you to check in and measure your behavior against this list until you make the right choices on a regular basis. Once you acknowledge that you can and will take responsibility for your feelings, you will be ready to look at your emotional self.

Looking at Your Emotional Self

Looking at your emotional self isn't an investigation into anyone's so-called defects. Don't be offended. We are here to help you, not hurt you. **Your entire emotional self affects your relationship with your adult children and how they relate to you, and it most certainly determines your response to sidelining.**

The purpose of this exploration is to see if there is anything impacting your emotional self that you aren't fully aware of and bring it to light, lest it impede your desire and ability to take responsibility for your feelings.

The Needy Factor

Lives change, and with it, so do the emotional needs and connections to our children. Oftentimes, we aren't even aware when we are coming across to others as needy. This short quiz will help you get a better sense of how your needy factor registers.

Do the following statements apply to you?

Statement	Yes	No
1) It is important that people express their appreciation of me.		
2) I get agitated and feel sorry for myself when situations don't go my way.		
3) I am surprised when people don't do nice things for me.		
4) I do best when I am rewarded or approved of.		
5) It is hard for me to be around people who don't recognize my good qualities.		
6) I tend to harbor resentment when people don't thank me or express their gratitude.		
7) I expect others to meet my emotional needs.		
8) I don't like it when someone isn't available.		
9) When people are critical of me, I get really upset.		
10) I like to feel wanted.		

Being needy can mean you want too much from others, are easily hurt, have insecurities, and basically aren't happy in your own skin. Parents whose happiness is too dependent on their kids and the way they are treated by them may be needy. Consequently, these parents become excessively hurt, unhappy, or angry when adult offspring don't do something for them.

Neediness is the last thing you want to communicate to your children. If you see yourself doing this, get some help. You should be able to be okay without your children making you feel happy.

There are degrees of neediness. We are all needy is some way. So if the majority of your responses are no, you probably aren't being perfectly honest with yourself or as happy as you could be.

The Happiness Factor

Let's review what we mean by happiness. **Happiness is a sense of overall contentment and comfort in your own skin that makes you feel like, "Yeah. I'm okay."**

And feeling okay is a very big step, Pat says. It's okay simply to be okay! You don't have to be deliriously happy or jumping for joy as long as you can do the following:

1) Get through all the crazy stuff that goes on in life
2) Appreciate the beauty in the simple things around you
3) Feel grateful
4) Appreciate that you are fine
5) Accept disappointment or sadness
6) Experience pleasure

If you can do these things, chances are you aren't one of the miserable people. Nonetheless, some individuals are naturally happier than others.

What's your disposition toward happiness? Respond to the statements below to get a read on your happiness gauge.

Statement	Yes	No
1) I question how worthwhile or valuable a person I am.		
2) I don't like spending time by myself.		
3) I don't like revealing my feelings to others.		
4) I am uncomfortable being myself in front of others.		

5) I am haunted by past mistakes.
6) I find it difficult to let go of something that has upset me.
7) I consciously try to make people like me.
8) My self-image is influenced by what others think of me.
9) My family members would describe me as somewhat unhappy.
10) I am not as okay with myself as I lead others to believe.

You have an issue with your happiness factor if most of your check marks are in the "Yes" column. Conversely, if all of your checks are in the "No" column, you may be hiding the truth from yourself. If you can't say, "Yeah, I'm okay," it's time for serious soul searching.

What does all of this have to do with your kids? Happier people are more pleasant to be around. If you aren't okay within yourself, it is likely that your children will play too big a role in your happiness. Furthermore if you are okay, you want to be nice.

Being nice helps every relationship!

The Miserable Factor
If you didn't score well on the happiness factor, you might find that you are squarely immersed in the miserable factor. This is not a healthy, happy place to be. In the event you cannot be objective with yourself, it might be fruitful to have a spouse or close friend answer the quiz questions with you in order to get a more accurate measurement of your miserable or happiness factors.

Respond to the statements below, and check the column that applies to you.

Statement	**Yes**	**No**
1) I find fault with people and am disappointed by them.		
2) I am frequently dissatisfied with circumstances.		
3) I dwell on the negatives.		
4) I might be described as a grouch.		
5) I tend to see the glass half empty rather than half full.		
6) My feelings correspond to how I perceive people treat me.		

7) I feel more sad than happy.
8) Bad things are always happening to me.
9) I rarely get what I want.
10) My life is not as happy as I hoped it would be.

You might exhibit more characteristics of being a miserable person than you thought. But don't despair. You can and should change your outlook. You have the power to do so. Failing to move on this point may mean you are more stuck in the muck of being a miserable person than you previously understood. And for goodness sake, don't say, "Who cares?"

Everyone around you does and is affected by your miserable factor, especially your adult children.

The Stress Factor

Little can make you as temporarily hot tempered, irritated, shortsighted, impatient, or inflexible as stress. You may not be aware that any one of the following factors creates internal stress and affects how you behave and respond to other individuals, especially close family members.

Take a moment to stop and think about whether you might be stressed by any one of the factors that affects our daily lives:

- Finances
- Health
- Grief
- Friendships
- Work
- Love relationships
- Children
- Grandchildren

Stress is best accommodated with tender loving care and compounded by outside aggravation. Revealing your stress to family members is a good idea.

Trying to alleviate stress will clear your mental resources and help put you in charge of your feelings.

The Control Factor

The excessive need to be in control is generally off putting and may make individuals who have an overactive control factor difficult people to have a comfortable relationship with. That's why it is prudent to measure your control factor and consider that of your close family members.

Test your control factor by responding to the following statements.

Statement	Yes	No
1) Are you irritated when someone says no to you?		
2) Do you feel smarter and superior to others?		
3) Do you think you can do a better job than most everyone else?		
4) Do you put your needs first?		
5) Are you miffed when you have to give into other people's points of view that you disagree with?		
6) Are you slow to concede an argument or point until it looks inevitable that you will lose?		
7) Do you expect others to comply with your demands?		
8) Do you prefer to be with people who will follow your lead?		
9) Do you enjoy having power over other people?		
10) Do you rarely do things you don't like to do?		

There is nothing wrong in having a strong sense of self. However, you know you may be dangerously close to overstepping your bounds when you allow little space for others to be themselves or share the lead. Chances are you are headed in that direction if you put more than a few check marks in the "Yes" column.

Having too big a control factor is normally deemed negative. However, it's never too late to whittle down a mega–control factor. We highly recommend that you do so. Wanting too much control was one of those qualities our adult kids found particularly negative and troublesome in parents. You don't want to be the cause of your own sidelining.

If the control issue applies more to your adult child than you, Chapter 8, "Talking It Over," should help you find a way to bring up this issue gently with your controlling offspring.

The Parental Maturity Factor

Parental maturity is another one of those telling factors that impacts relationships with adult offspring and alleviates missteps on the part of parents. A better score on parental maturity (first discussed in chapter 5) should lessen the frequency of conflicts. And if it doesn't, at least you will be able to say you have acted in a mature fashion and feel justified not taking on the blame.

Here you go again. Respond to the statements below.

Statement	Yes	No
1) I expect respect, and I give respect.		
2) I accept my adult children for who they are.		
3) My adult children are independent and have their own lives.		
4) I try to be open-minded when their values and decisions do not necessarily reflect my own.		
5) I try not to impose my expectations on them.		
6) I accept the fact that my children may be right, and at times, I am wrong too.		
7) I am willing to work on our relationship to make it better and more comfortable for everyone.		
8) I have relinquished my parental rights.		
9) I try to be loving, caring, and supportive, despite our differences.		
10) I can accept the fact that my relationship with my adult children may not be everything I had hoped it would be.		

It is probably safe to say that no one has a perfect score of ten yeses! But the fewer the noes, the closer you are to reaching a desirable level of parental maturity.

Gaining and maintaining parental maturity is an ongoing process affected by all of our inner factors, outside influences, and the behavior of our adult children. Nonetheless, achieving parental maturity is a worthwhile factor to work on improving each and every day. The greater your maturity level, the better your chances are for achieving a higher happiness quotient and a better relationship with your offspring.

Looking for Hidden Dynamics

There are still subtle, hidden factors deep inside that may prevent you from liberating yourself from the painful sting of sidelining. Identifying these factors gives us greater insight into our reactions and what we need to do to respond in a more beneficial fashion.

Individuals, especially those who don't want to take responsibility for their feelings, won't readily gravitate to this process. People who don't have this resistance and are more open-minded will see the value in looking for hidden factors.

The good news is that you can still profit from the guidelines and information in our book without digging deeper. You can always go deeper. Self-discovery is a never-ending process.

The two examples that follow demonstrate how another mother and I enlightened ourselves and achieved a more satisfying level of happiness after looking deeper within ourselves. There is always value looking inside oneself. For me, learning to take responsibility for my feelings has been a game changer!

Getting in Touch with My Feelings

No doubt I felt hurt and abandoned that my daughters did not express regret when they were unable to settle near my husband and me once they married.

I remember finding a letter to my parents I wrote while living in California telling them how I hoped someday to be able to move back home.

Equally, I felt unloved when they fought or found fault with me, especially during the period my husband and I were dedicated on a daily basis to our four sick, elderly parents, who resided only minutes away. I was constantly angry.

Let's look at two old, sticky, somewhat-benign instances that remain stuck in my mind. Admittedly, we have been through much tougher, more serious, and painful times that need not be dwelt upon. Nonetheless, these less stressful situations serve my purpose of investigation.

Several years ago, my younger daughter expressed near panic and disapproval that her father and I were even thinking of changing our city of residence to be near her and our older daughter. Equally trying was a vacation with my older daughter and her family when I was not allowed to sleep with my then-three-year-old grandson. We always had the most fun together doing this during my visits. We had treats, told stories, and snuggled before my grandson would climb into the top trundle bed to fall asleep. Why my daughter had chosen to deny both of us that pleasure when he had to sleep in a room by himself on a rollaway bed, I couldn't begin to understand.

Like so many parents and grandparents out there, I was insulted and annoyed by both of my daughters' responses that felt disrespectful, mean, and meant to punish me for some unknown infraction. Initially, there were simple revelations that helped define my self-imposed grief. My ego was bruised, for sure. I wanted my way and didn't like having my authority challenged. And on some level, I felt cheated that I was being denied the daily expressions of love my husband and I afforded our four sick parents. The anger that sapped my energy and denied my happiness would not abate. Where was this anger coming from?

Psychologists insist that fear precipitates anger. So I delved into myself for answers.

Was I afraid that in old age, my husband and I would be alone without our children close at hand to provide comfort, pleasure, and supervision? I suppose so, but I think more to the point was the fear and disappointment that they didn't reciprocate my love for them.

On a deeper level, I discovered that much of what angered me was more likely my disappointment that my children didn't behave toward me the way I hoped and expected they would. I wanted them to have that enormous love I felt toward my father and expressed by gladly giving him free reign with my children. I enjoyed every moment I spent with my father and appreciated all the amazing things he did for me. I never stopped him from filling my girls' mouths with candy or denying any other pleasure he took in indulging them. Any rules I had did not extend to his interaction with my girls. I was thrilled when he couldn't get enough of them. It was my gift to him and his to me.

So where was that unconditional, delicious love I was anticipating from my girls?

Was I perhaps really not as lovable I wished to be? Maybe I was too needy, a quality I found annoying in my mom. Or did I maybe feel guilt-ridden for mistakes made raising my daughters?

Did I feel remorse for punishing my older daughter when she lied by not allowing her to attend a good friend's fabulous bar mitzvah party? I must have still felt a little twinge of guilt. When the bar mitzvah boy got married, I insisted my daughter go to the wedding, flew to her home to take care of my infant grandson for the weekend, and asked, "Will that absolve me of my crime, and could we call it even?"

And was I perhaps even haunted by guilt the time I told my younger daughter in front of company to think before she spoke? Were those my big revelations?

Maybe I made mistakes that deemed me unworthy of the respect and love I sought. Is that all there was? Most likely, no. There are two sides to the story.

However, for the moment, I am content with this level of exploration; I have acquired the ability to oversee my reactions and don't sense the need to go deeper. Making the conscious choice to be less reactive and more vigilant choosing how I wish to feel is sufficient and has made me a happier mom. Also, it isn't an issue anymore whether my three-year-old grandson will be allowed to sleep with me. He is now sixteen.

It simply doesn't matter if my kids don't abide by my priorities, share my core values, visit as often as I would like, or occasionally speak in an unpleasant way to me. None of it is as devastating as it used to be. Although there is a bottom line that neither of my girls would be wise to cross.

For now, there is no more sulking, anger or boring my friends with my complaints when things don't go as I hoped. It isn't worth the toll sidelining might take on me, and it doesn't do any good! I permit myself to feel hurt and miffed for the moment. I cannot spare more precious moments that I could use doing something else.

I have begun to recognize that life just isn't the way I want it to be and that just because I gave so much as a parent, I may not get what I think is the equivalent back. And furthermore, if I made mistakes, so be it. Didn't we all? It was time to let go of any ridiculous guilt and unrealistic expectations that prevented me from reacting more gracefully to any and all rebuffs.

There is a peacefulness now that reigns over me that wasn't present before I did my work. I am more content and easier to live with.

Do our issues past and present mean that we aren't a loving and caring family? No. I can count on my kids to be there if I really need them, and they know I am always there for them should they need me. We have wonderful moments together, and I love them as much or more than before.

Do they love us? I would bet yes. Do they always like us? Probably not. Do they always behave how I want them to? No. Do they always do what I want? No. Can I change them? No. Are they responsible for how they feel about me? Yes. Am I okay with that? Sure. Is there more work that could be done to reduce ongoing, underlying friction and improve our mutual level of enjoyment? Probably yes. Have we talked it all out? I doubt it.

Can I live with all of this? Yes. I have control over only myself—and sometimes my West Highland terrier.

Donna's Epiphany

Donna was Pat's patient several years ago. She drove three hours to her office one day to reveal her trials, tribulations, and eventual epiphany to me. The following is her story in her own words.

"My husband and I run a successful insurance business together and did so when the girls were growing up. Our office was in our home. We were always around. My daughters were my whole life. We were totally devoted parents and did a lot for the girls. They didn't pay one penny for their education. One of the girls was particularly close to her father. The other kind of went her own way once she left for college at eighteen and minimally communicated with us afterward.

"Our relationship with our adult kids was entirely one sided. I would go visit my grandchildren as often as I liked and help my daughter out, although she would be snarky to me. I remember one time, this really ticked me off. Her in-laws, who she and her husband support, had just left. She is wonderful to them and told me she was so sad they had to leave. They are way up there, and we are way down here. We don't ask for anything but respect, which we didn't get. It eats at you.

"When my husband and I had martial problems a number of years ago, my daughters were angry that I put up with their dad's shenanigans. He drank too much and got hooked on painkillers because of a serious injury from an automobile accident. They didn't like his behavior and insinuated that I ought to leave him but then backed off. I think they knew they would lose me if they kept this up.

"We had a particularly bad family visit at our bungalow in Vail; my husband's substance abuse caused a huge problem. Instead of helping, my daughter and son-in-law made matters worse for me. They verbally went after my husband, who was already feeling down on himself. Then my high-powered son-in-law, whom I didn't like because of the way he treated my daughter, yelled and criticized me on the beach.

"I would have liked some sympathy and understanding. Instead, they brought a gift of chocolates, thinking that a present was all I needed. We didn't talk for nine months after that.

"I felt totally left out of their lives. When their father underwent two surgeries, neither daughter came to help me or ask how I was. I needed someone to ask me that. I would have answered that I was falling apart and would like for someone to help me out. All I could think was, 'You brats!'

"That's when I went to Pat.

"What I learned was that I hated the way I was raised. My mother wasn't interested in us. She was into herself, and my father ran around a lot. I had a poor sense of self-worth, despite my business success. Equally—if not more importantly—I learned that I didn't have to be dependent on anyone, nor did I want to feel responsible for my thirty-something children anymore. I had been needy and wanted them to fill my emotional vacuum.

"Once I realized all this, I had an aha moment. I didn't have to prove anything anymore. Screw it! I knew I had done everything I could for my children and grandchildren. I wasn't going to let my daughters rent space in my mind with their issues, and I wasn't going to put up with any crap anymore. If they didn't want to be around me, fine. I knew I was okay. I consciously allowed myself to separate from my adult children. They were no longer the center of my life. I was ready to enjoy myself and focus on the positive. I started taking care of myself, lost thirty-five pounds, and ran a marathon.

"Eventually, I put it all out in the open with the girls. I said I had had enough of their nastiness and judgments. Were they willing to start over with a clean plate? Yes. I listened to what they had to say and never once said 'You are wrong' or 'You did this,' even though I may have thought it in my mind.

"Then it was my turn. I laid down the rules. There would be no more screaming at me, no more horrible letters making mincemeat out of me if I did something they didn't like, and no more blowups. I simply wasn't willing to put myself in an uncomfortable position any longer. I have tasted a new freedom, and I like it!"

Connect the Dots into a Full Circle

The steps of inquiry provided will guide you further into your own self-discovery. Try it, and see what discoveries await.

Step #1

Write down at least four "Hate Feelings" you have with regard to your children's behavior. For example, "I hate it when my adult kid disrespects me, dismisses what I have to say or is patronizing; I hate it when my kid's spouse treats us as if we aren't important."

1. _____

_____

_____

_____

2. _____

_____

_____

_____

3. _____

_____

_____

_____

4. _____

_____

_____

_____

Step #2

Catch and record your emotional reactions when your adult kids act out the behaviors you hate.

1. _____

_____

_____

_____

2. _____

_____

_____

_____

3. _____

_____

_____

_____

4. _____

_____

_____

_____

Step #3

Try to list a minimum of five thoughts that might be fostering your emotional reaction. Guess if you are not sure.

1. _____

_____

_____

_____

2. _____

_____

_____

_____

3. _____

_____

_____

_____

4. _____

_____

_____

_____

Step #4

Come up with at least two old experiences or situations that somehow feel connected to your current reactions and thoughts.

1. _____

_____

_____

_____

2. _____

_____

_____

_____

What is bugging you deep down may not readily boil up to the surface. Just keep working on it. The good thing is that you can begin on a better path and reduce the negative effects of sidelining once you assume responsibility for your own reactions.

You are, after all, a work in progress.

What's Next?

You should be sufficiently in tune with yourself and in control of your thoughts and feelings to maximize an opportunity to engage your adult children in fruitful dialogue by now. The art of talking it over and gaining mutual understanding is spelled out for you in chapter 8.

CHAPTER 8

Talking It Over—When, Where, Why, and How

Talking things over with your adult children is always a good first step. **The vital part of wanting to talk is that it creates hope.**

We know many of you don't believe it is possible to have an honest dialogue with your adult children. Ninety-nine percent of the responses on our questionnaires clearly indicated that parents of adult children rarely feel they can communicate openly with them.

Parents avoid having "the talk" because they are fearful of what might be said. The anticipation of all the awful, negative stuff that might come up derails attempts to talk seriously. It's a huge problem, and no one should underestimate just how hard it is for both parents and adult kids to have the big talk. It can be really scary, particularly when the most casual comment has the potential to be perceived incorrectly and spark negative responses.

Adult kids today are bogged down by their assumption that nearly everything a parent says to them is judgmental or has a hidden agenda. What else could explain this explosive exchange between a well-meaning mom and her daughter on the day of her wedding?

Mom: You and Jake are such a wonderful match. He is so calming.
Daughter: You bitch!

Fortunately, the bride's mom accepted the remark as something laughable instead of outrageous, chalked it up to wedding jitters, and smilingly took her seat at the ceremony. This wasn't the time or place to make a point or have a confrontation.

When this mom did opt to begin "the talk," she was well prepared. You will be too.

If your attempts to have constructive conversations with adult children have failed in the past, trying again is an important option. The relationship tools and keen insights acquired reading this book thus far should enable you to begin a fresh and more productive dialogue. However, don't initiate the conversation until you have attained some mastery over the steps outlined for you in this chapter.

Step One: Determine Your Motives

Check your motives with the right and wrong ones listed below before you take a step toward formulating your talk. **The wrong motives will sabotage all efforts to create a healing conversation.** Therefore, do not even begin to move on to helpful, general guidelines or preparation for a talk until your motives are solidly vetted.

The Wrong Motives

One of the dad's interviewed was at a bursting point when we met. "I just want to call up my son and tell him what I think of him," he said. "Why shouldn't he know all the things he has done to aggravate and upset me for the last fifteen years?"

Needless to say, this poor man was on the wrong track!

Make sure none of the items in this list influences your desire to have "the talk."

You are not ready to start discussing serious issues with your adult kids if you want to do any of the following:

- Inflict guilt or punishment
- Lay blame
- List old grievances, transgressions, and hurts

- Reveal grudges
- Assuage your anger
- Seek sympathy or pity

The Right Motives

The motives that should drive your desire to have a serious conversation with your adult son or daughter will reap the most benefits from your talk. These motives include wanting to do the following:

- Build a better relationship
- Share feelings
- Exchange understandings
- Resolve conflicts
- Create intimacy
- Show empathy and caring

Record Your Motives

To make sure your motives aren't tainted, write them down precisely and clearly before you move on.

My motives are:

1) _____

_____

2) _____

_____

3) _____

_____

4) _____

_____

5) _____

_____

6) _____

_____

Step Two: State Your Goals, and Formulate a Plan

Now that your motives have been identified, stating your goals should be relatively easy. Adhering to these goals will keep you on track. Determining what you should say or how and where to say it is a more daunting task. We'll get to that soon enough.

Goal Tending

You should have a clear picture regarding what kinds of goals are achievable. To be even more precise, differentiate between your short-term and long-term goals.

We have provided a list of goals for you that are intended to start you thinking. Either pick from those below, or, better yet, add some of your own.

The following might be worthy short-term goals for your talk:

1. Have a non-confrontational, pleasant, and positive conversation that moves away from past negativity
2. Take the opportunity to state your concerns
3. Have an opportunity to ask if your adult child thinks you can have a better relationship
4. Learn more about what is going on in your child's life
5. Demonstrate your love and caring

6. Come across as honest and flexible
7. Express your limits, if appropriate
8. Find that talking is good for you
9. Work out a plan that addresses the issues about which you are both concerned
10. Agree to return to this conversation if necessary

Your talk may include the following worthy long-term goals:

1. Create greater mutual understanding
2. Nurture a more loving, caring, and compassionate family through talking
3. Put an end to sidelining or negative behavior
4. Help your child see your needs
5. Learn to pay more attention to your child's needs
6. Work through ongoing conflicts
7. Open the door to more honest talks
8. Build intimacy
9. Learn to enjoy each other's uniqueness and create a mutually fun, enjoyable relationship
10. Resolve the issues that have been bugging you and work out a plan to make your relationship better

Set Your Goals
Your short-term goals

1. _____

_____

2. _____

_____

3. _____

_____

4. _____

_____

Your long-term goals

1. _____

_____

_____

_____

2. _____

_____

_____

_____

3. _____

_____

_____

_____

4. _____

_____

_____

_____

Step Three: Be Ready to Seize the Right Moment

You are getting a plethora of instructions, so this next one may come as a surprise. The best plan for the where and when to have your talk is not necessarily formally planned.

The Spontaneous Discourse

A prearranged date and time is often met with too much anticipation, infers a possible lecture, and sounds like a summit between two adversaries. This is precisely the atmosphere you want to avoid!

What is preferable is spontaneity when there is calm and privacy that invites conversation. This could be driving in the car, taking a walk, having lunch, or sitting and relaxing with a glass of wine. This way, it takes the weight off what you are saying and makes it seem like no big deal.

This recommendation doesn't preclude careful preparation—just the opposite!

Be ready to seize the appropriate moment when it arises.

Readiness and Timing Are Key

If you have done all of your preparation in advance and are just waiting for the right opening, when it arrives, you won't be speechless. Your well-thought-out conversational plan will be in place to make the most of the moment.

If the time is right, you will know it. It will seem natural to broach the subject you have been mulling over in your mind.

If, on the other hand, the moment never arrives, you might have to delicately call a summit; preferably phrase it as a lunch or dinner date to discuss something of importance.

A Personal Point of View

Looking back at my own experiences, I can tell you without reservation that the spontaneous message or talk is the most productive route when you have thought out the issue in advance. I am willing to share one of my best and worst efforts with you.

Obviously, the good effort reflects my prior consideration and readiness to address the issue when it arose. The poor effort unfortunately reflects a knee-jerk reaction, with little or no control over my thoughts and feelings and certainly no preplanned consideration of the situation at hand.

A good effort:

My younger daughter, who lives a good six hours away from us, was telling me some of her summer plans, which included travel to visit her in-laws and a family break at the eastern seashore. I didn't say in a snide way as I might have, "Well, I certainly hope you have time to make it home to be with us. I would have expected that you wanted to spend time with me and your father."

I had been thinking about how to address this delicate matter without sounding jealous, angry, or blaming. Consequently, I was prepared to communicate my message in a much less confrontational and more diplomatic way. "Your father and I are feeling a little neglected and lonely. I know your schedule is tight, but could you think about coming for a visit?"

She piped in quickly. "You are right. We haven't been to see you in a while. Let's find a date we can come in."

It is a given that she is amenable to open conversation. Nonetheless, she could have responded poorly if the tone and plea hadn't been tailored to be acceptable.

A Poor Effort:

My husband and I were visiting both of our daughters, who live in the same city about a half hour from each other. I was finding it very difficult trying to get everyone together for a family dinner at a locale that was unanimously pleasing. Nothing was working.

Here we were in town feeling as if both of the girls should work their weekend dinner plans to accommodate us after we made the effort to travel and visit each of them. The longer this back-and-forth texting and phone calling went on, the angrier and more upset I became.

Before I calmed myself down, I demanded the girls come for coffee within the hour to the hotel. I thought, in a public place, at least none of us would make too big of a scene. Wrong.

They knew before they got there that mom was on the warpath, and before I knew it, I was spewing out old and new grievances. I was not in control of my feelings, thoughts, reactions, or my mouth! I had not considered this carefully. In other words, I did not have the benefit of all the knowledge contained in this or previous chapters!

Needless to say, there were tears and accusations. The dark cloud that hung over our entire visit outlasted the storm, and we never did have that big family dinner.

Obviously, my emergency meeting did more harm than good and accomplished nothing.

Step Four: Hone In on the Topic

Nothing should be off limits when it comes to talking to your adult offspring, as long as it is presented in an empathetic and compassionate way. It isn't in anyone's best interest to keep secrets.

Nonetheless, be wary of beating a dead horse. Once you speak your peace, that's it. Don't keep harping on the same issues. So before you jump into a discussion with your adult child, hone in on a topic, and vet it thoroughly.

Consider the Topic Inside and Out

Although everything is legitimately up for discussion, consider the following issues before you select your topic. Make sure you won't be pouring gasoline on a bonfire. Consider these questions before you broach the topic:

1) How do I think my child will respond to this topic?

_____

_____

_____

2) What should I avoid?

_____

_____

_____

3) Might this topic lead to an argument?

_____

_____

_____

4) What is the baggage load on this topic?

_____

_____

_____

5) Is this my issue or my kid's?

_____

_____

_____

6) What long-term or unresolved problems might be behind the topic I wish to discuss?

_____

_____

_____

7) What is the least problematical way in which I can broach this subject?

_____

_____

_____

8) Will I be able to control myself discussing this and keep my cool?

_____

_____

_____

Evaluate or Modify Your Topic

Look back on your answers. They should not deter you from talking, but they can give you a pretty good indication of whether or not the topic at hand is too loaded with probable negative repercussions. Until you are almost certain that you can derive something positive out of discussing the issue, steer clear of it for the time being.

Topics may not be the problem; how you present them could be.

Step Five: Define Your Rules of Engagement

Remember the old adage "Think before you speak." Well, the time to do that is before you engage your adult child in a serious talk.

Your Number One Rule

Do not whine and complain about how you are treated when you have your talk with your adult children. Rather, choose your words carefully, deliver them in a congenial tone, and focus on how your child might feel.

Here is an example of what we mean. Imagine you have a difficult daughter-in-law who treats you like an unwelcome outsider and puts the kibosh on family holidays or vacations, grandchildren's sleepovers, and Sunday dinners. You may think you have the right to state exactly what's on your mind to your son. Wrong!

Even if you believe it, do not say, "Your wife is a selfish woman who cares only about being with her parents. She doesn't even pretend to like us. Do you know how awful, sad, and disrespected that makes us feel?"

Instead, make it about your kids, stow the complaints, try some diplomacy, be respectful and caring, speak kindly, and ask, "Are you comfortable having Mom and I stay at your house when we visit next week? We think it may be uncomfortable for Mary and make things difficult for you. We don't want to create a problem."

More Rules That Benefit Your Engagement

We have discovered guidelines that get the discussion going and render the best results. We encourage you to abide by the following recommendations.

Do:

1) Engage in a discourse
2) Respect your children's point of view
3) Invite your kids to express how they feel
4) Ask for what you wish for
5) Take responsibility for your actions and feelings
6) Apologize when it is warranted
7) Remain in control of your emotions
8) Be diplomatic, direct, honest, caring, calm, courteous, open-minded, and receptive
9) Speak in positives, and say what you need to
10) Be a good listener

Don't:

1) Give a lecture
2) Demand that your adult kids behave according to your dictates

3) Start finger pointing or use "blamey" stuff

4) Speak in negatives, sound angry, or become sarcastic

5) Make comparisons (they sounds judgmental)

6) Use combustible words like *want, should, supposed to, you, deserve, have to,* or *wrong*

7) Keep focused on a manageable topic

8) Act or sound like a victim

9) Scream, cry, swear, accuse, overreact, or engage in theatrics

10) Bring up past transgressions that happened ages ago

Step Six: Anticipate Your Opening Lines

The first words out of your mouth influence everything that follows, how your message will be received, and whether or not your talk gets off the ground. That's why we suggest you give your opening lines considerable thought.

Potential Opening Lines

We are giving you a few opening lines. Use one of these, or make up your own as long as they are comfortable, clear, and cannot be misconstrued. Pay attention to the differences between the messages in the two columns.

No negative messages allowed!

Say	*Don't Say*
I may have misunderstood you.	You pissed me off.
I hope we can get along better.	We have a horrid relationship.
Can we try and solve our differences?	You and I don't think the same at all.
I love it when we can be upfront.	I am afraid to tell you anything.
I love you.	Sometimes I can't stand you.
Do you have time to help me with a problem?	You never have time for me, but I want to talk to you.

Write Your Own Opening Lines

The best lines are the ones that you compose yourself. They should be comfortable for you to say, sound natural, and reflect your own personality.

Write several opening lines you might draw upon to start your talk.

1) _____

_____

_____

2) _____

_____

_____

3) _____

_____

_____

4) _____

_____

_____

Be Ready-Practice Your Lines

Rehearsing your opening, writing notes, and even role-playing are ways to help make sure you get your talk off on the right track. Of course, you don't want to sit down with your children and pull out a notebook or a piece of paper with a prepared speech on it. But practicing words and phrases that best express your message are more likely to roll off your tongue the way you intended if previously positioned in your mind.

This is just one more tip to make your talk fruitful.

Step Seven: Prepare Yourself to Be a Good Listener

Being a good listener may take practice and self-control. It is critical when talking with your adult children. **A good listener is completely engaged in what the other person is saying. He or she is responsive and interested, which demonstrates respect for who is speaking.**

If you aren't naturally a good listener, it's a skill worth developing.

What Good Listeners Do

A good listener wants to learn and take in information. There is no way to reach greater understanding or gain new insights without being a good listener.

Here are some suggestions to improve your listening skills:

- Not only hear the words, but interpret what is being communicated by them
- Stay open-minded
- Be willing to see a situation through the other person's eyes
- Do not become defensive
- Demonstrate empathy and understanding by smiling
- Focus entirely on what is being said without being judgmental
- Observe the other person to gauge their needs and feelings
- Do not interrupt
- Wait your turn to speak
- Make sure that the other person's responses indicate he or she understands what you have said
- Review in your mind everything that you learned in the conversation

A Good Listener Quiz

The next time you have a conversation with an old or new friend, ask yourself these questions:

1) Did I learn anything from our exchange?
2) What didn't I know about this person that I just learned?
3) Did I monopolize the conversation?
4) Did I ask questions in response to comments or information given?
5) Did the other person enjoy talking with me?

Failing the Test

If you cannot state anything you learned about the topic or the person you were speaking with, you probably weren't a particularly good listener.

You most definitely failed the good listener quiz if you monopolized the conversation and did not ask any questions about the other person. In that case, the answer to question five will most likely be a no!

Step Eight: Monitor Your Talk

You will need to carefully monitor and take charge of the direction of your conversation to cover your agenda and reach the goals you established for your serious talk. This takes self-control, focus, skill, and practice. However, if you have mastered steps one through seven, this shouldn't be too difficult a challenge.

Use Words and Phrases as Cues

Simple words and phrases can help guide the conversation, keep you on track, encourage clarity and understanding, and keep things rolling. The following useful questions are good tools to have at your disposal:

- I may not be hearing you clearly or getting your message straight. Could you please tell me that again?

- I think this is what you said. Do I have it right?
- Could we stay on this point a little longer and come back to this other subject later, please?
- Is this how you feel?
- Is it helpful talking about this?
- Am I making any sense to you?
- Do you see where I am coming from?
- It feels so good to talk like this. Do you agree?
- Is there anything you want to tell me?

Know How to Conclude the Talk

One of your goals is to keep the door open for future talks. The way you conclude your talk often determines whether or not there will be a next one. The pointers below work toward ensuring future meaningful dialogues:

1) Ask you adult child if he or she feels better now that you have talked
2) Find a positive comment on which to end
3) Ask if you can do this again
4) Express how good it felt to talk on this level
5) Never leave angry
6) Say good-bye with a hug or a loving message

Step Nine: Create a Post-Talk Evaluation Notebook

Just because the talk is over doesn't mean your job is done.

To make sure you didn't miss anything or to help plan future talks, keep a notebook, date your entries, and record you impressions. Here is what to consider:

1) Did the talk go well? If not, why not? If yes, why?

_____

_____

_____

_____

2) What could I have done to better facilitate the conversation?

_____

_____

_____

_____

3) What was implied but not stated outright by my adult child?

_____

_____

_____

_____

4) What wasn't discussed that I thought or hoped would be?

_____

_____

_____

_____

5) What did I hear that might have expanded my understanding of my adult child's position?

_____

_____

_____

_____

6) What did I learn?

_____

_____

_____

_____

7) What might my child have learned about me?

_____

_____

_____

_____

8) What should I have said?

_____

_____

_____

_____

9) What questions did I fail to ask?

_____

_____

_____

_____

10) What do I think would be beneficial to continue to discuss or ask the next time?

_____

_____

_____

_____

When Talking Won't Do Any Good

As much as we hate to admit it, there are times and circumstances when talking won't necessarily improve your situation. In that case, you will have to rely on the wisdom of your inner self, the control you have acquired over your own feelings, and your healthy determination to be happy.

Think twice—better yet, three times—before initiating a talk if you have already tried to introduce the topic over and over again without success. Be particularly mindful if you think the outcome of a talk could potentially be negative and do more harm than good.

What's Next?

For a variety of reasons, some of you who have read this far may still be experiencing some resistance to change. Chapter 9 will address that problem and help you get beyond it. There is no reason to resist change unless you want to remain unhappy.

CHAPTER 9

Working with Your Resistance to Change

Parenting is a selfless job with a lifelong, oversized emotional invest-ment that renders moms and dads vulnerable to the painful sting of sidelining from their adult children. Nonetheless, parents need not be subject to ongoing distress once they become aware of the origins of their discomfort or unhappiness, are mindful of their interactions with their adult children, and rid themselves of any resistance to change.

Pain Invites Change
The fact is that pain actually invites change. Individuals who resist mak-ing changes are mired in their own issues and often consciously or sub-consciously enjoy being victims.

Their resistance is expressed by an unwillingness to compromise, accept other points of view, give up control, deal with their reality, or take responsi-bility for their thoughts and feelings. If you exhibit any resistance to change, now is the time to work through it.

Here are a few important reminders:

- The best antidote to pain is changing your thoughts and reactions by taking responsibility for your feelings
- We are not negating the fact that your adult children can act miserably to you, whether it is a lack of respect or failure to value your participa-tion in their lives

▪ Be that as it may, you are the one and only person who can use your pain as an impetus for positive change

What Is Preventing You from Changing?

You can't make your kids change, so the onus is on you to change in a way that enables you to take charge and move toward a more satisfying future. Don't think we are suggesting that you acquiesce to every infraction. We believe in bottom lines and will get to them in chapter 10. For the moment, stick with us until you discover what is preventing you from making changes that could ease your pain.

Your progress toward change could be impeded by any one of the mindsets below or the issues presented in the section "Accepting Family Reality on All Fronts." Carefully consider which of the factors presented in this chapter have stonewalled your attempt to exchange pain for gain.

If you are unable to do this yourself, you may need a coach or therapist. Never hesitate to get the help you need!

Are You Mired in Your Own Issues?

The issues we are talking about make people feel badly about themselves on some level and prevent them from experimenting with change. They encompass the following:

a) A lack of self-esteem
b) Frequent unhappiness
c) A victim mentality
d) Closed-mindedness
e) Neediness
f) Stress
g) Fear of looking within
h) An unwillingness to take responsibility for feelings

We have discussed and tested you for signs of these issues elsewhere in the book. Now is the time to come to terms with them. Do not allow these matters to linger. They directly affect your ability to see things in a new light and advance toward a more comfortable relationship with your adult children. Review each characteristic that strikes a nerve with you.

Are You Stuck on What Is Right and Wrong?

Whether a behavior is right or wrong is often a subjective determination influenced by personal opinions and beliefs. For instance, **all the things we think our children should do for or with us are not necessarily a matter of right or wrong.**

There is not a moral imperative for adult kids to spend time with parents, invite their folks for dinner, include them in social outings, spend every holiday together, take dad's advice, make life easier for mom, fulfill their parents' needs, or place as much importance upon their mother and father as they do their spouse or their children. If you are too rigid in your assessment of what is right and wrong and can't get past these labels, you may be missing the opportunity to value your adult children for who they are. In this case, you are hurting yourself and need to consider whether you are stuck because of your own self-interest, personal issues, or stubbornness.

Take Gwen for example. Each of her three children lived in a different city. When her husband was diagnosed with cancer, her two daughters came for their father's surgery and left while he was still in the hospital. On the date of his release a week later, Gwen's son flew into town to help get his dad home and stayed for the weekend.

"Once Ted and I were settled back home, it was as if nothing had ever happened," Gwen said. "It was another week before we got a phone call from any of the children. I know they have their jobs and family responsibilities at home, but you have only two parents, and who knows for how long. I just couldn't understand where they were coming from. That isn't how they were raised; that isn't how you are supposed to treat parents. It just isn't.

"When my son and younger daughter came home for a long weekend together three months later, I had to bite my tongue to keep from telling them what I thought of their selfishness. As for my oldest daughter, she called once a week until Ted's treatments were over but never showed up once. I can't forgive her. What's wrong with these kids? Do they expect to show love and support only if Ted is close to death? I am heartbroken."

Gwen had enough on her shoulders without adding the burden of pain incurred from her adult children's behavior. **Accepting her adult children's behaviors as mistakes, rather than unfulfilled imperatives, might have promoted a search for greater understanding and helped Gwen feel less aggravated.**

Being less rigid in judging what is right or wrong can encourage parents to seek the reasons behind their adult children's mistakes, enable honest conversation, ease painful feelings of rejection, and dispense with compiling more angry grudges.

Everyone makes mistakes, including you and your adult children! So what else is new?

Are You Unwilling to Take the High Road?
Taking the high road is choosing a path that is bigger than you and your feelings. It requires getting over your own grievances and letting them go. Traveling down this road necessitates the following:

1) Pleasing someone else before yourself
2) Putting aside your own reactions
3) Curtailing your self-interest
4) Foregoing criticism or judgments
5) Being compassionate, understanding, kind, and empathetic
6) Not making a big deal out of everything
7) Letting go of old grievances
8) Being nice even when you don't want to be

Jeanie's daughter-in-law had been nasty and distant for years, refusing to interact with her husband's family. When the daughter-in-law surprisingly joined the family for a night out and then expressed having a wonderful time, Jeanie said she wanted to reply, "Well, you could have had this all along if you had been nice." Instead Jeanie took the high road and told her daughter-in-law, "I am so happy you decided to join us."

"Why would I want to start a fight or upset my son? We can't go back and relive those years. What good would it do to make a snide remark? I need to accept her for who she is," Jeanie said. "Our relationship will never be the way I hoped it would be. That probably makes my son happier. He doesn't have to feel torn leaving her at home all the time to spend time with his family."

The benefits of taking the high road are bountiful. If you haven't done it in a while, try it! It makes you feel good, strong, and loving. Not to mention, it has a positive effect on those around you.

Accepting Family Reality on All Fronts

In Chapter 5, we discussed how loving family members interact. Now it is time to view your family behavior from different perspectives.

The point of this entire discussion is to encourage you to evaluate your family fairly and not judge your adult children on the basis of such lofty ideals that they can't help coming up short. **You need to be realistic about who your family is, what you want from them, and how you can accept what they are able to give.**

Front #1: Family Outlook

Real families aren't perfect, even the seemingly flawless ones! We constantly ran into this reality in interviews and follow-up conversations with parents.

Questionnaires came back from both a husband and wife. Each indicated that their relationship with their married daughter was a ten. When casual conversation ensued at a later date, it became apparent this dad wasn't as completely satisfied as he had previously noted. Although he was unwilling to discuss the intimate details, the tears that welled up in his eyes when he spoke about his son-in-law were sufficient to indicate that everything wasn't as perfect as he had reported. That's okay. There's no shame in not having the ideal family.

It is not unusual for parents to feel they have to display the perfect family. It's what we tend to expect and feel pressured into having. We believe it is a reflection of our own goodness if our family is good. It is not, Pat says.

The problem comes into play when you cannot reconcile this perfect version of family with your reality, and this fuels unhappiness, pain, anger, discontent, and all the other feelings we have identified with sidelining. Accepting that all families—yours included—are not perfect and never will be makes way for changes in attitudes that will serve you and your adult children better.

Parents who stop fantasizing about how their family could be are more likely to begin accepting what cannot be changed, graciously appreciate what they do get from their children, and stop aggravating themselves over what could be.

Front #2: Parental Maturity

We have already introduced you to the concept of parental maturity, accepting your children for who they are, in Chapter 5. Mastering that can be difficult, especially when you aren't aware of just how deeply the ways in which you think your children ought to behave are embedded in your vision.

Thoughts like "I can't believe my son puts up with his wife's constant demands," or "Why doesn't my daughter leave her husband already? I wouldn't stand for his behavior for a day" indicate a lack of parental maturity and improper expectations that adult children will respond to situations in a manner that is yours.

If you have achieved true parental maturity, you accept behavior that is counter to your particular position unless it does harm to your adult child or others.

Front #3: Patience and Tolerance

Patience and tolerance are two behaviors that keep you out of trouble. This is particularly true when applied to your newly married offspring or his or her

155

partner. Failure to be tolerant and patient can cause problems that haunt you for years.

Numerous parents complained that once their adult children became engaged or formed a serious love relationship, they practically became estranged. There was no time for mom, dad, or the family, and there was no place in their lives for helpful suggestions or conversational intimacy.

Years ago, I was told by a very smart mother, "It takes a while before newlyweds realize they can love more than one person." And **it takes time for you to understand and cultivate a satisfying relationship with the stranger who has been brought into your family.** Be flexible and congenial until you get to know this person.

Extending patience to the newlyweds as they formulate "couplehood" is wise. Keep your feelings under wraps lest they provoke misunderstandings and feelings of interference. Neither of which you want.

A father with a very logical, mathematical mind admitted that he felt particularly distant from his son after he married. He felt uncomfortable in his adult child's home and could not relax due to his new daughter-in-law's standoffishness. Although he was distraught and saddened, he said, "I will see how it goes and allow them to calibrate their married relationship."

His willingness to extend patience and exhibit tolerance positioned him well for the arrival of his grandchild. Without creating any earlier controversies or hard feelings, his daughter-in-law learned how to welcome him into her home and now readily shares her son with her husband's parents.

Front #4: Parent-Child Relationships

The manner in which you relate to the following specific factors may greatly affect the satisfaction you derive from your adult child–parent relationship. Dealing with each of these factors thoroughly provides invaluable insights, helps you remove unrealistic expectations, and enables you to avoid further disappointment or pain from feeling being sidelined.

Take the time to carefully consider each of the following:

1) Intimacy

It is true that open, honest exchanges encourage intimacy and understanding, but intimacy is rarely achieved across the board and simply may not be possible with a particular adult child. There are those topics sons or daughters deem off limits, and there are issues adult children have not resolved within themselves that can make it uncomfortable for them to reveal their honest feelings.

Your relationship, however, does not have to be predicated upon the closeness derived from intimate exchanges. These exchanges may not occur. That's okay. Accepting this lessens disappointment and reduces any pressure you may be putting on your child to be more forthcoming. It also opens up the potential for other avenues of enjoyment together.

Table talk can be fun and special in its own way. No matter how mundane the conversation is, it ultimately provides an opportunity for you to model empathy and compassion that can result in building intimacy.

2) Sharing Core Values

Core values are internal, fundamental beliefs that guide one's behavior and actions. **Sharing the same core values as family members enhances mutual understanding and provides consensus on how to treat one another.**

When you and your adult children hold the same core values (such as family comes first, family members should respect and love each other, and each family member ought to be treated with dignity, empathy, care, and compassion), then the likelihood of a less conflicted relationship is greater.

Of course, similarly, interpreting how to demonstrate these values is equally important. In other words, how you project that family comes first may well be interpreted differently among family members. But as long as the shared values are present, one has a greater opportunity of working out better ways to put them into play.

On the other hand, without shared family values like the ones above, it is much more difficult to arrive at a place where the family connection is loving and caring.

3) Loving without Liking

We encountered poster children who loved but did not like their parents. The same is true for parents; some loved but did not necessarily like their children—at least not every part of them. The truth be told, most parents seemed less likely to dislike their children than the other way around. In either case, it is rare that either parent or child dislikes everything about the other. It does not have to be a matter of all or nothing.

We are assuming the lack of compatibility is because kids don't like something specific about their parents or what they are doing. **If your goal is to achieve a more compatible relationship, focus on the positives, and work around the negatives.** Here's how to do it:

1) Try to determine what the issue is
2) Correct what you can or want to
3) Accept that it is okay if your kids don't like everything about you
4) Don't make this a big deal

Front #5: Parental Roles

Parental roles with adult children can be tricky. Don't overstep adult boundaries. Appropriate roles for parents of adult children include being:

1) Loving, supportive, and positive
2) Kind and caring
3) Helpful in times of need
4) A good listener, confident, and sounding board
5) A provider of unconditional love
6) An independent person
7) A teacher and role model for standards and lessons

We have intentionally excluded "being a friend" from the list of appropriate roles. Thinking that being friends is desirable is a mistake. What it may indicate is that you are seeking your child's approval, Pat suggests.

Wanting to be your child's friend misses the point. You have been your child's caregiver, unconditional supporter, and provider in times of need. Being friends does not begin to encompass the role parents play. The parental role goes way beyond friendships.

Front #6: New Possibilities

The most prevalent tensions revealed by our study's participants dealt directly or indirectly with their adult children's spouses or partners. They were seen as either sideliners themselves or the cause of their adult child's sidelining. So it seemed liked a promising place to help readers open up their minds and look more in-depth at what may be getting in the way of their adult child–parent relationship.

What you uncover when looking for a deeper understanding of your adult child's partner's behavior can be of huge benefit to you. It may also provide important revelations about your own child.

As long as the kids are married or together, it is well worth your effort to work on finding positive connections!

A Case for Not Stirring the Pot from the Get-Go

Don't be the cause of trouble, especially when you can avoid it.

Mia, a forty-five-year-old divorced mother of two, developed a serious love relationship with Jake, and her parents had a fit. They disapproved of him entirely and told her so. When Jake gave Mia an engagement ring and wanted to discuss his plans with her parents, they refused to talk to him. That was a big mistake. Never refuse to talk! Once Mia's parents realized they might have been too harsh, Jake was no longer in the talking mood. He had already determined they were way too interfering and insulting. To this day, Mia maintains a relationship with her parents, but Jake has no relationship with them at all. This makes it awkward when Mia's parents come to visit.

Putting your adult child in the middle gets you nowhere. Be careful! At times, parents aren't aware that that is precisely what they are doing.

The Case of the Mega-Difficult Daughter-in-Law

Pat firmly believes it isn't always intentional when daughters-in-law push in-laws away, and she has proof. Marla's argumentative, brash, and nasty veneer repeatedly drove her mother-in-law to tears. Marla didn't dislike her mother-in-law as much as she was emotionally unfit to relate to her in a nicer way.

Marla was raised in a family in which she was relegated to third place, behind her twin brother and sister. They were loved in a way she felt she wasn't. To make a long story short, her self-esteem and self-confidence levels were in the dumpster. When her mother-in-law arrived on the scene, she became the recipient of all the pent-up anguish Marla harbored for her own mother. Had Marla's mother-in-law been more aware of this behind-the-scenes dynamic, things might have taken a more positive turn.

Remember, there is always a reason people behave the way they do.

The Case of the Dominant Son-in-Law

Carole's daughter changed after she said, "I do." Time with and access to her daughter diminished slowly over the years. Plans made with excitement and enthusiasm one day were broken the next. Their relationship became strained, superficial, and problematic.

Carole repeatedly begged her reluctant daughter to visit a therapist with her to work out their problems. Fortunately, she eventually acquiesced.

Many of the problems that had erupted in this mother-daughter relation-ship were the result of an overactive, dominant son-in-law. Carole was never aware that it was her son-in-law who refused to allow his family to be taken on trips by her and her husband. She did sense his annoyance when gifts of com-puters or electronic games were given to the grandchildren at Christmas, but she never connected this with why both families couldn't celebrate together or why her daughter rarely came to her home for the holidays. Carole was devastated thinking that her daughter simply didn't want to be a part of the family anymore.

The hidden truth discovered in therapy was that her son-in-law, the domi-nant marriage partner, usually managed to get his way. He disliked his in-laws because of their ability to do things for his children that he and his parents could not financially swing. And he didn't like anyone to infringe on his leisure time.

Instead of feeling hurt and pulling away from her daughter as she had done in the past, these revelations encouraged Carole to help her daughter become a stronger individual. Her daughter in turn was grateful to be able to tell her mother honestly why she couldn't always accept invitations. Eventually she gained her own voice, asserted her will, and took the family trips she wanted to partake in even though it meant leaving her husband at home.

Your Family Assessment and Reaction

Now that you have read this chapter, let's see how well you have absorbed the essence of its message and applied it to your personal situation.

Put a check in the appropriate column that best describes your answer to the following questions.

Question	**Yes**	**No**
1) Do you have a realistic view of family life in general?		
2) Is your parental maturity level where it should be?		
3) Do you practice patience and tolerance when relating to your adult children and their spouses?		
4) Have you accepted that you may not be able to have the close relationship with our adult offspring that you hoped for?		
5) Do you fulfill the roles of adult parenthood sufficiently?		
6) Are you able to open your mind enough to garner more insight to your adult child and his or her spouse?		

A checkmark in the "No" column indicates an area where you need to improve your sense of reality and acceptance of your current adult child–parent relationship. **Keep in mind that we don't always get what we want in life. You will be happier once you fully accept that! And most likely, so will your adult children.**

What's Next?

The future is up to you. You are ready to use all of the personal insights, wisdom, suggestions, and tools we have brought to your attention to set wise boundaries and mark your bottom lines in the final chapter. You deserve to make these determinations now that you are open-minded, understand yourself better, and aren't so dependent upon your children for your happiness.

A concise outline that succinctly shows the immediate steps that will best serve you when confronted with sidelining also awaits you. It should serve as a handy reference. Once you learn to confront sidelining in a more practical manner, it will get easier every time you are faced with more. It is called building resilience.

CHAPTER 10

Managing Your Future

Throughout this book, you have gained valuable knowledge about yourself, learned ways to look at your kids and their behavior in a different light, and been instructed in techniques that can turn you into a happier, more content person. Now it is time to put it all together.

If you use the recommended guidelines in this book and take responsibility for your feelings, you will be empowered to formulate necessary boundaries, assert your bottom line, resolve issues, and feel a sense of freedom of spirit and peace of mind that eluded you before now.

Setting Your Boundaries

Boundaries are essential in every relationship. They help to:

1) Determine healthy give and take
2) Maintain individual well-being
3) Set up guidelines for interaction
4) Ensure control over your own life
5) Influence your actions and responses

During our research and interview process, four distinct areas in which parents were having difficulty setting beneficial boundaries were identified. These exacerbated sidelining and sabotaged their chances of resolving issues with their adult children. Perhaps one of the four problem areas applies to you and requires a reset.

Don't be put off of establishing your own boundaries, even though they could conceivably draw criticism from friends and family. Avoid those people who second-guess your wisdom when it comes to setting limits with your adult children. You need to be strong, believe in yourself, and when in doubt, seek outside professional assistance.

Attachment and Boundaries

We are aware that kids can hurt us like no one else in our lives. The parent-child relationship is not like any other. One can never replace a child, but you can replace a friend or even a husband.

Nonetheless, pay attention to this critical message: **if your overall sense of happiness is dependent on the well-being of your adult children, how they treat you, or whether they wish to be close to you, then you need to start thinking about some healthy separation and boundaries.**

This can be more of a problem for mothers than fathers. For example, every time a particular mom came back from seeing her children, she reported feeling miserable, useless, depressed and sorry for herself because she no longer felt an integral part of her kids' lives.

Many of the women whom we heard similar complaints from lived close to their adult children. Proximity to their adult children was not the issue, but boundaries and degrees of separation were. Being overly attached to your adult children may cause huge heartache. The only antidote is to separate yourself sufficiently.

The loss of what once was—that unimaginable connection and reliance of a child on a parent—may require a period of grieving to get over. To overcome this, you must be mindful of these feelings, understand your disappointment over the natural change in your relationship, and do what you can to create your own internal source of happiness.

Dollars-and-Cents Boundaries

In an era when adult kids feel entitled to their parent's financial resources and parents recognize the difficultly their children are having achieving economic security, the prevailing question is this: "Should I or shouldn't I dole out the dough?"

Confused parents everywhere ponder this. Each situation is different, requires serious consideration, and should be evaluated on the specific circumstances. There is no hard-and-fast rule that applies to everyone!

There are, however, two important questions that will help you determine whether or not to hand over the money.

1) "What is my motivation for giving money?"

If your motivation for giving money to your adult children is to maintain a sense of dependence that feeds your desire to be needed, make them indebted to you, control their decision making, appease them, or buy their love and attention, it is probably time to start setting up some serious boundaries. None of these are healthy reasons for writing out a check.

2) "Will giving money cause more harm than good?"

When giving encourages codependence, prevents adult children from assuming responsibility for themselves, funds substance abuse habits, assuages parental guilt, prevents an individual from addressing serious issues in their own lives, or takes advantage of you and weakens your financial security, stop! None of these are good reasons to give!

Good reasons to provide financial assistance generally include the following:

- Offering lifeline support
- Creating meaningful opportunities that are out of reach for adult children or their kids
- Sharing resources with your family that allows you to spend time together

For example, paying the rent to give your grandchildren a roof over their heads, helping hardworking adult children down on their luck, paying for promising substance-abuse programs, assisting with educational costs, or financing appreciated family vacations with you all qualify as good reasons to help out.

Nothing can replace objectivity and sound judgment when it comes to determining your course of action surrounding giving. Make sure your evaluation is systematic and sound. If you require confirmation, seek advice from a trusted friend, your accountant, or a professional.

Substance Abuse and Tough Love Boundaries

Earlier, we noted the rising, alarming rate of substance abuse among the population of adult children we are focused on. Substance abuse by an adult child is a really, really hard issue for parents to tackle, Pat says. Parents express a lot of guilt and may have to look at themselves to make sure they aren't enabling their children by giving them money. Whether or not to institute tough love remains a puzzling issue and requires serious consideration that often necessitates getting help from professionals who deal with addiction issues.

The litmus test for determining beneficial boundaries or invoking tough love must ultimately be determined by whether it is done because you care about what is best for your child, not because you are angry or overly sympathetic.

Kicking your substance-abusing adult child out of your house because you can't stand it anymore may not be what is in the best interest of your child. But paying the rent when it is not in the best interest of a substance abuser may be just as damaging.

Ultimately, you must know yourself and your child. Recognize that when you are dealing with substance abusers, you may be in disagreement about what is in their best interest. But you need to trust yourself! You don't want to be pushed around by a substance abuser. Everyone has to know where to draw their own line and when to seek assistance.

Boundaries for Self-Preservation

Removing yourself from your adult child's life temporarily or for a prolonged period of time may be a matter of self-defense. This is particularly true of parents who are way too accommodating, will do anything to please or appease their adult child, and are treated without respect or kindness.

Don't be afraid to say no. You are entitled to your own life. If you have difficulty erecting boundaries that protect you, this is a problem that needs extra attention and counseling. Your motivation for not doing this may be tied to unresolved issues, many of which we may have covered in preceding chapters.

There is no valor in unnecessarily sacrificing yourself for your adult child. Remember, we already established that being kind includes being kind to yourself.

Your Bottom Line

A bottom line is an individual's most basic position and firm limit to a situation or behavior that produces an outcome when crossed. Despite everything you have tried, you may feel yourself getting closer to your bottom line if you have reached a point where you will no longer tolerate certain behaviors or attitudes. Many bottom lines seem to be delivered in the heat of a moment, but chances are, they have been simmering over a period of time and determined before reaching a boiling point.

Crossing a bottom line need not lead to a complete dissolution of your relationship. Sometimes simply revealing your bottom line does enough to rectify the situation. We will provide you with several complete examples of bottom lines to clarify the picture.

Moving toward Your Bottom Line

Each individual must assess and determine his or her bottom line in the end. Nonetheless, when nearing your bottom line, consider the following criteria. You may not be activating a bottom line when it could be prudent, or you may be employing a bottom line when it might be premature.

Make your decision after reading everything we have to say on bottom lines. You will know for sure if you have justifiably reached your bottom line when you:

1) Are the recipient of excessive nasty behavior
2) Determine you just can't go on like this anymore
3) Repeatedly try to work out problems, but it does no good
4) Are abused, used, and totally compromised
5) Find your relationship has become toxic
6) Are constantly unhappy due to your adult children
7) Acknowledge that your children do not share or respect your core values
8) Are treated as if you have no right to your own feelings
9) No longer experience kind or caring treatment

A Note of Caution
Bottom lines can be positive and negative. Therefore, to make sure they stay positive, consider whether or not:

1) You arrived at your bottom line fairly and objectively
2) The consequence you established for crossing this line is something you can live with
3) Your adult child is aware that he or she has crossed your bottom line

Three Different Examples of Crossing That Bottom Line
Reading about parents whose kids have seriously breached their bottom line will provide clarity.

Example #1: A Bottom Line with an Ultimatum Attached
Eleanor admits she probably waited too long before laying down the law, stating her bottom line, and issuing an ultimatum. For ten years, she and her

husband put up with what she called abuse at the hands of her son and his wife, who dominated the relationship.

"I enabled the situation because I was afraid to lose the grandchildren if I didn't continue to be nice. Just months ago, we paid for daycare and preschool. My son and his wife never let us know when there was a school program and never invited us on Mother's Day, Father's Day, or Thanksgiving, even though they had her whole family over. My daughter-in-law would ask me to pick up my grandson and take him to an after-school lesson. I would get to their house, and they wouldn't be there. I blamed my daughter-in-law the most, but my son knew better too. He was not raised in that kind of household.

"Finally, one day, something snapped. I went over to their house and said I wanted to speak to my son privately. I told him I would not allow him to treat me this way anymore and that I had extended both hands to him. I let him know that I thought his father and I were just a checkbook to him. I then walked out of the house and slammed the door. I never knew what went on after I left. I did write my son a letter, listing all the things that we had done to help him get through life and stating that I would not put up with his behavior in the future, even if it meant not seeing his children.

"We never discussed it beyond that, but things changed drastically. For the past several years, everything has been wonderful."

No doubt this young man "got" his mother's bottom line.

Example #2: A Bottom Line with No Recourse

When Pamela reached her bottom line with her daughter-in-law, there was no going back. She was finished! Pamela acknowledged that if her son and his wife had children, she might not have acted in the same way. But since that was not the case, and because she was confident that she would be able to maintain a close relationship with her son despite calling it quits with his wife, Pamela proceeded to do what she felt was best for her.

"In the beginning, my daughter-in-law liked me. When her parents couldn't give a wedding, we hosted one in our home. It wasn't until after her mother died that she became upset with me. Actually, she was hateful.

"For several years, I tried to pacify her the best I could. No matter what she accused me of, I treated her like one of my own daughters. I would send her things when I went shopping, just like I did my girls. But she started calling me up and saying I was trying to change her or that she knew I wasn't happy Jason married her. Increasingly, she became more and difficult and harangued me on the phone.

"Still, when I called my son at home and she answered, or when we travelled across country to visit them, I was nice. My husband and I never stayed at their house and always extended a warm invitation for her to accompany Jason to dinner with us or anything else we might be doing. She never came and ignored us completely.

"One day, after they had been married a number of years, she called and started hollering at me about the same old things. I finally told her she was welcome to believe whatever she wanted but that I was tired of trying to convince her otherwise and that I refused to listen to her anymore. I said I wasn't going to go there or be harangued anymore. Then I told her I was going to hang up and that we needn't have any conversation again.

"I did not call my son immediately. Rather, the next time I spoke with him, I told him what had transpired. He said I should have called him, but I told him there was no way I was putting him in the middle. I think my son and she are happy together in their own way. I have no idea if they ever discussed what happened or what arrangement they came to. He comes to visit on his own and sometimes meets us for a few days at a vacation spot. I know he loves his father and me, and he knows we love him dearly. I think he understands our struggle completely and has never tried to persuade us to change things.

"When I call to speak with my son at his home and his wife answers, I say, 'Hello, may I speak to Jason?' That's it. She will hand him the phone. I do believe he told her that there was no way he would sever his relationship with us.

"I don't hold any grudges against her. Grudges aren't worth it in this life. But I simply could not withstand this aggravation anymore. If she wanted to resume a relationship on civil terms, I would be amenable. However, she has never made any overtures in that direction. My belief is that if I can change something, I will. If I cannot, I have to live with it the best way I can, and that's what I have done."

Pamela pulled out her bottom line and was serious about it not being crossed again.

Example #3: A Bottom Line with No Room for Compromise

Jennifer has a substance-abusing daughter whom she has supported by paying for treatment and by helping to raise her three children. Jennifer paid for things, but she took the precaution of directly sending checks to the electric company rather than handing over sums of cash to her daughter.

"You don't want to put money into the hands of a substance abuser. My daughter lies and says that she is clean and sober, but I know this is not the case. When she moved to another state, taking her children with her, and became even more deceitful and verbally abusive to me, I had to completely cut ties and stop all communication directly with her. I always send holiday cards so that she knows I am thinking of her. Most importantly, I wanted to make sure that my grandchildren, who were in their teens, knew that they could always call me and that I would always be there to support them. One of the three children did come to live with me.

"Now, several years later, Jennifer's daughter has started trying to communicate with her.

"I will respond briefly as long as my daughter is respectful and not abusive. During hard times, I have paid some bills for her. My line is clearly drawn, and she seems to know it. My grandchildren, however, remain my primary concern."

Is It Time to Annul Your Relationship with Your Adult Child?

We certainly do not advocate ending relationships with adult children. However, the cruel realization is that in some instances, estrangement is the only viable path. Usually, the child, not the parent, initiates this. But parents have just cause when their adult child's behavior becomes poisonous and harmful enough to them that there is no other recourse.

No matter who decides to pull away from the relationship, it is a difficult set of circumstances for parents to live with. Parents should not feel guilty. Rather, they need to work through a grieving process, much like one would after a death. If they can't move on, and the pain does not subside significantly after a period of time, professional help should be sought.

No doubt some element of grief will always be there. But the parents' primary job is to accept the separation and get on with life. **Being estranged from one's adult child should not prevent parents from experiencing pleasure.**

Hopefully, after reading this book and putting into play what we have presented, your relationship will improve so that the idea of estrangement is not even remotely present in your thoughts.

Responding to Sidelining With a Compact Three-Step Method

To make sure you can visualize a healthy, general response to future sidelining, we are providing you with a quick reference tool in the form of a brief outline. This is a bare-bones outline. The meat is in every page of this guide! Through disciplined repetition and practice, however, your reaction to trouble should become more spontaneous over time.

I. In a Nutshell, How to React to Sidelining

A) Remember you are in charge and have all the tools to confront future sidelining!

B) Take responsibility for how you feel, and don't blame others.

C) Choose how you want to feel.

D) Do not react in a thoughtless, rash, or angry manner.

E) Act in a kind and caring manner that in no way compromises you.

II. Look for Answers before You Act

A) Attempt to gain greater insight into what happened before taking a path of action.

B) Make a preliminary determination about whether this is your issue or your adult child's.

C) Consider what might be affecting the sideliner.

III. Work Out a Thoughtful Plan

A) Using all the tools you have acquired to evaluate the situation, begin to consider a way to solve the problem that is satisfying to you and does not compromise your well-being.

B) You may decide to do the following:

1. Ignore the sidelining event entirely and decide it is not a big deal
2. Vent
3. Talk it out
4. Go for a temporary "time-out" or time away from the stress of dealing with your kids until you feel refreshed and equipped to address their sidelining
5. Seek greater emotional separation from your child
6. Take a look at your boundaries, and reset
7. Serve up your bottom line
8. Call it quits, and say enough is enough
9. Find a coach or therapist if you cannot determine a plan for yourself

Building Resilience

Resilience is the ability to minimize stress, adapt, and recover quickly when something bad happens. It is a natural by-product of healthy responses that are repeated over time.

You are building resilience each time you respond to sidelining by taking responsibility for your feelings and behaving less reactively. You can also train yourself to be more resilient in the face of trouble, even when that trouble arises with your adult children.

Resilience Is a Learned Skill

According to neuroscientists, research and brain imaging prove that specific emotional responses, such as anger, feeling sorry for oneself, or blaming others, prevent the growth of brain resilience. On the flip side, **repeated and positive responses to difficult situations develop new pathways that encourage the growth of resilience and better health.**

Applying this model to sidelining, we suggest that parents:

1) Let go of painful, angry responses tainted by a victim mindset
2) Take thoughtful control of their feelings
3) Deploy the improved responses to their adult children's behavior that we have described throughout this book

Tips for Developing More Resilience

The following list is taken from a variety of sources. Some of these tips reinforce the points we have made and bear repeating. Each tip is worthwhile for improving your ability to quickly bounce back to a happier track in the face of adversity.

To help improve your resilient quotient, do the following:

- Take responsibility for your feelings
- Don't beat yourself up
- Develop close family relationships and friendships
- Practice a positive outlook
- Find meaning in bad situations
- Discover what makes you strong
- Believe in yourself and your ability to solve problems
- Find a strong role model

- Meditate
- Get rid of negative thoughts and feelings

The more resilience you build, the less sidelining will affect you. That's the goal, right? Absolutely!

What's Next? Sending You Off on Your Own and Wishing You Good Luck!

You can never totally wipe the slate clean, pretend your disagreements and disappointments with your adult children did not occur, or ignore your shared history. But you can put the past into perspective, begin to approach the future in an enlightened manner, and chart your own course. The future is yours to choose.

Your choice is between remaining miserable and unhappy or opting for something better. It is entirely in your hands! Rely on the following mantra each time you begin to waver.

I am a caring, kind person who speaks in a positive way, tries to understand my adult child in all situations, determines my own feelings, and is responsible for my own happiness. When my adult children sideline me or have a negative reaction to me, it is their issue. I refuse to allow their behavior to make me feel like a victim.

About the Authors

Rosanne Rosen is an author and life coach who focuses on family and love relationships. She received a Bachelor of Science degree in social work and a master's degree in history from The Ohio State University. Ms. Rosen is the author of over two hundred newspaper and magazine articles as well as five other relationship books: *Marriage Secrets*, *The Living Together Trap*, *The Idiot's Guide to Handling a Breakup*, *The Idiot's Guide to Living Together*, and *The Idiot's Guide to Mothers and Daughters*.

Ms. Rosen has interviewed hundreds of individuals for her books and appeared on national TV and radio. Ms. Rosen and her husband are the parents of two adult daughters and have four grandchildren.

Rosanne can be contacted at RosanneRosen.com and is available for coaching services related to sidelining and other topics covered in her books.

Dr. Patricia James, PhD, is a psychologist with a dual degree in clinical and developmental psychology.

She received her PhD at The Ohio State University in Columbus, Ohio. Before going into private practice, Dr. James was a clinical instructor of psychology at Children's Hospital in Columbus, Ohio, teaching graduate and medical students from The Ohio State University. Dr. James has been in private practice for over thirty-five years and specializes in treating families, children, and adults.

Dr. James has one daughter and two grandsons.